RPJ

HYMNS & ARIAS

MAX BOYCE, singer-songwriter, poet and entertainer, was born in 1943 in the village of Glynneath, south Wales, where he still lives with his wife, Jean. They have two daughters, Cathy and Rhiannon, and two granddaughters, Rhosyn Alaw and Evelyn Grace.

Despite the fact that his father was killed in a mining explosion a month before Max was born, Max went on to work underground in the local colliery at the age of sixteen – a profession he remained in for over a decade.

After releasing two records on a small Welsh label, in 1973 he recorded his iconic breakthrough album, *Live at Treorchy*, which went on to sell over half a million copies. Several gold and silver records followed, including *We All Had Doctors' Papers*, which went to number one in the UK Albums Chart and is still the only comedy album to attain this coveted position. He has since toured the world, playing sell-out concerts in some of the world's great venues, including the London Palladium, Sydney Opera House and the Royal Albert Hall.

His BBC television series attracted over twenty million viewers and merely confirmed Max's popularity among young and old alike. His exploits following the Dallas Cowboys, the American rodeo circuit and the 1985 World Elephant Polo Championship in Nepal were chronicled in the bestselling book *In the Mad Pursuit of Applause*.

In 1999, he was awarded an MBE, which he received from Prince Charles at Cardiff Castle, and in 2013 he received the Freedom of the Borough of Neath and Port Talbot, following in the footsteps of Sir Richard Burton and Sir Anthony Hopkins. In 2022, there are plans to unveil a bronze life-size statue of Max in his hometown – a fitting and deserved tribute to a modern-day folk hero whose poems, songs and stories have become part of Welsh legend.

Where is the boy that I used to know,
Where did he run to, where did he go?

MAX BOYCE
HYMNS & ARIAS
THE SELECTED POEMS, SONGS AND STORIES

Parthian Books, Cardigan SA43 1ED

www.parthianbooks.com

Contents © Max Boyce 2021

All Rights Reserved

ISBN 978-1-913640-95-8

Edited by Robert Harries

Cover and interior design by Syncopated Pandemonium

Cover photographs by Luke Hodgkins

Photograph and illustration credits:

Rhys Padarn Jones/Orielodl (www.orielodl.com): endpapers; Max Boyce: ii, 17; Handshake Ltd: vii, 1, 10, 21, 39, 89–90, 100, 104, 106, 113, 117, 125, 130–172, 180; Matthew Horwood: viii; Jeremy Wood: xii; Gren: 2–8, 12–14, 18–19, 22–23, 26–27, 34, 42–44, 70, 76–77, 82–83, 98–99, 101–103, 111, 114, 174; Jimmy Giddings: 9, 123; PA Images/Alamy Stock Photo: 24–25, 47; INchendio on iStock by Getty: 30; Darryl (Gren) Jones: 30–31; David Davies/PA Wire: 37; Action Images/ Paul Harding Livepic: 41; Mirrorpix: 46; Jeff Morgan 07/Alamy Stock Photo: 51; Anne Cakebread: 52–53, 64; Mirrorpix/ Reach Licensing: 55; Fran Evans (www.franevans.com): 56, 63, 69, 72–73; Trinity Mirror/Mirrorpix/Alamy Stock Photo: 61; Mike Straw on Unsplash: 66; Russell Stanley: 74; graham bell/Alamy Stock Photo: 75; Mael BALLAND on Unsplash: 77; Leila Cutler/Alamy Stock Photo: 78; REUTERS/Alamy Stock Photo: 85; Immo Wegmann on Unsplash: 87; ID 5738817 © Scol22 | Dreamstime.com: 93; EMI: 96–97; Jonny Gios on Unsplash: 105; Character © 1982 Petalcraft Demonstrations Ltd: 108; tirc83 on iStock by Getty: 116; Jeff Morgan 04/Alamy Stock Photo: 178–79; Alison Carman: 179.

All attempts have been made to track down copyright holders where possible; uncredited material is reproduced in this book under the terms of fair use, but both publisher and author endeavour to correct and offer full credit in future editions.

Printed and bound by Gomer Press, Llandysul

Published with the financial support of the Welsh Books Council.

British Library Cataloguing in Publication Data

A cataloguing record for this book is available from the British Library.

CONTENTS

FOREWORD

This collection of my poems, songs and stories is something I have promised to write for a very long time, but I never found the time or the dedication to apply myself to the task of 'carving words like jewels'.

There was also the haunting realisation that my words would have a sort of finality, no longer able to leave their final resting place, disturbed only by the turning page. A sanctuary where they would listen quietly to their own silence and where their only visitors were strangers . . .

My thanks then must go to Richard Davies and Parthian Books for believing in my work, and to Robert Harries for his endless patience in painstakingly transcribing my handwritten manuscripts, which at times looked as if a spider had fallen into a bottle of ink, climbed back out and crawled drunkenly across the pages.

This being so, we got it completed, and the returned 'copy' looked like someone else's work that was infinitely better than my own.

I've called the collection *Hymns & Arias* because it's the title of a song I wrote hurriedly some fifty years ago, little thinking it would stand the test of time and be sung on the terraces of Cardiff Arms Park, the Millennium (now Principality) and Liberty (now Swansea.com) stadiums, where the faithful carry their songs like a soldier carries his rifle to war . . .

In more recent times I have used the chorus and tune of 'Hymns and Arias' to tell the story of some memorable moments that I was privileged to be in attendance for, from Wales versus England at Wembley Stadium in 1999, 'When a Tear Fell from Graham Henry's Eye',

> And so farewell to Wembley and to this foreign clime
> Next year we're back in Cardiff, if they finish it on time
> They say it's got a sliding roof that they can move away
> They'll slide it back when Wales attack so God can watch us play

to the opening concert of the Welsh Assembly in Cardiff Bay,

> Here's to our assembly that they've built along this shore
> They built it here in Cardiff . . . though Cardiff voted NO!

to the Wales rugby team's arduous training camp regime before the World Cup in South Africa,

> Why take the team to Doha I just can't understand
> The camels there have flip-flops on to walk upon the sand
> And those 'cryogenic' chambers, their worth is still in doubt
> They had to use the warm-up games to thaw some players out . . . !

and then Swansea City AFC's first home game in the Premier League, against Wigan,

> Here's to all you Wigan fans, it does seem strange to me
> That you used to have a pier but you haven't got a sea . . .

These little vignettes would never have a claim to permanence, for their time with us was fleeting, but for a short while they had their time in the sun and held a truth that was honest and authentic.

Some of the songs in this book took a lot longer to write. Songs such as 'Rhondda Grey', 'Duw! It's Hard', 'The Incredible Plan' and 'When Just the Tide Went Out'.

They lay unfinished in cupboards and drawers, on the back of bits of paper, fearing the dark, worrying that no one would come and find them. Till one day they were brought out blinking into the daylight, inspired by no more than a passing thought or word or by some unknown alchemy.

I have likened my 'Craft and Sullen Art' to the skill of a blacksmith who puts his work into the heat of the furnace, waits till it's white hot and then bends it to his will. When it has cooled, he repeats the process.

In much the same way, I put my songs and stories into the furnace of performance, altering a line here and changing a word there until I am satisfied they are the best they can be and best suited to the gifts I may or may not have.

These, then, are my poems, songs and stories formed in the embers of that furnace.

I know many people will recognise themselves in the pages of this book, for they have travelled the same journey, walked the same paths. They have shared the same hopes and dreams, the joys and despair, and prayed to the same gods.

Many of these moments are revisited in the 'Hymns and Arias' of this book.

Those moments turn the well-thumbed pages of a book I have yet to take back . . .

M. B.
August 2021

To Jean, Cathy, Rhiannon, Rhosyn and Evelyn
Fy Ffortiwn (My fortune)

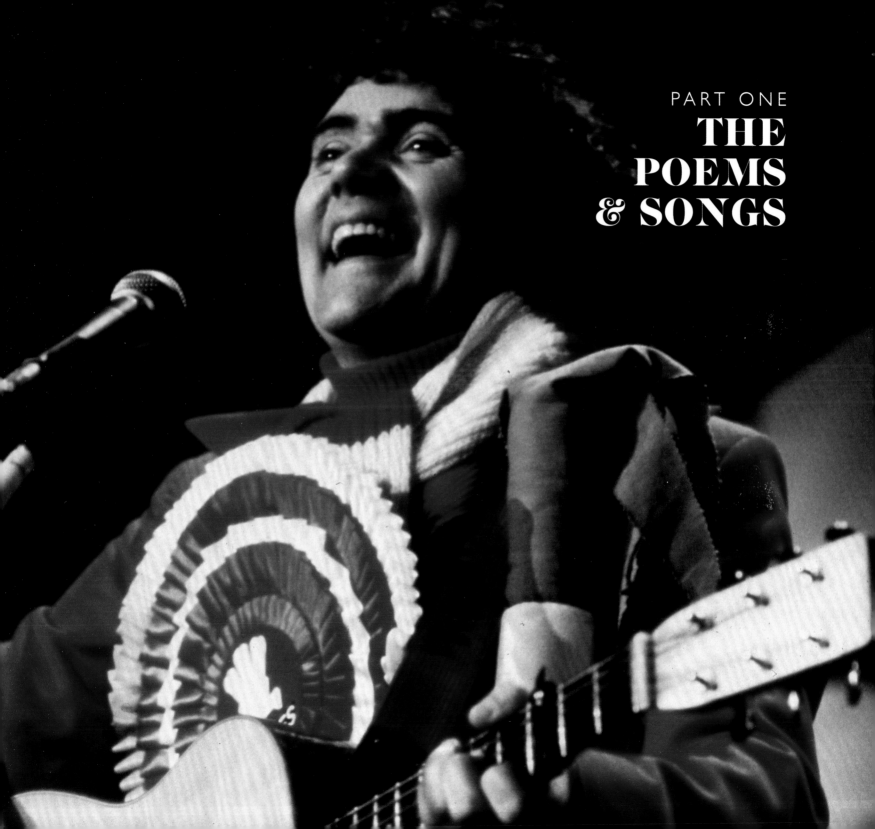

PART ONE
THE POEMS & SONGS

HYMNS AND ARIAS

'Hymns and Arias' is a song which tells of the trip that thousands of Welshmen make once every two years to see Wales play England at Twickenham.

When it was first sung by the crowd at Cardiff Arms Park someone wrote, 'Cwm Rhondda and Calon Lân have found a companion.'

It was undoubtedly one of the greatest moments of my life, and it still gives me a great thrill wherever and whenever I hear it sung. I shall always remember that first time . . . I was being interviewed by Frank Bough on 'Grandstand' in front of the North Enclosure at Cardiff Arms Park before the Wales–England international. (Earlier that week I had bought a long, very expensive suede coat with a big fur collar to wear on the programme.)

The crowd recognised me and started to sing 'Hymns and Arias'. When the interview was over, I ran around to the BBC van and telephoned home. My mother answered and I said, 'Mam! Did you see "Grandstand" and hear the singing?'

'Yes,' she replied.

'What did you think of it?' I asked excitedly.

'Oh!' she said. 'Your coat looked lovely.'

CHORUS
And we were singing hymns and arias,
'Land of my Fathers', 'Ar hyd y nos'.*

We paid our weekly shilling for that January trip:
A long weekend in London, aye, without a bit of kip.
There's a seat reserved for beer by the boys from Abercarn:
There's beer, pontoon, crisps and fags and a croakin' 'Calon Lân'.

Into Paddington we did roll with an empty crate of ale.
Will had lost at cards and now his *Western Mail*'s for sale.
But Will is very happy though his money all has gone:
He swapped five photos of his wife for one of Barry John.

We got to Twickers early and were jostled in the crowd;
Planted leeks and dragons, looked for toilet all around.
So many there we couldn't budge – twisted legs and pale:
I'm ashamed we used a bottle that once held bitter ale.

Wales defeated England in a fast and open game.
We sang 'Cwm Rhondda' and 'Delilah', damn, they sounded both the same.
We sympathised with an Englishman whose team was doomed to fail.
So we gave him that old bottle, that once held bitter ale!

He started singing hymns and arias,
'Land of my Fathers', 'Ar hyd y nos'.

---

* 'Ar hyd y nos' = 'All through the night' (not 'Harry's got a horse').

So it's down to Soho for the night, to the girls with the shiny
    beads;
That shy away in corners just to tempt a Welshman's needs.
One said to Will from a doorway dark, damn, she didn't have
    much on.
But Will knew what she wanted, aye . . . his photo of Barry John!

'Cos she was singing hymns and arias,
'Land of my Fathers', 'Ar hyd y nos'.

I GAVE MY LOVE A DEBENTURE

Some years ago a debenture scheme was introduced by the Welsh Rugby Union. It took the form of tickets put on sale to help raise money for ground improvements at Cardiff Arms Park.

These tickets, or debentures as they are known, guarantee the owner the same seat in the stand for all internationals at Cardiff. They were initially sold at the reasonable price of £50 but have since escalated terrifically in value, £8,500 having been offered recently for four.

Their present worth, however, is perhaps best illustrated by the song, 'I Gave My Love a Debenture'.

I met her in the Con. Club in Pontypool;
The public bar was crowded so I offered her my stool.
I said, 'Fair lass, pray tarry. Come stay awhile with me.
And I'll give you my debenture – Block A, Row 3.'

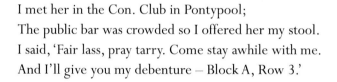

Her eyes were pale as lyder; her hair was long and black.
The only thing that spoiled her was she wore a plastic mac.
I said, 'Fair lass, pray tarry. Come sit upon my knee.'
She thought awhile and then she smiled. I thought,
'Ho, ho, he, he, hee hee hee!'

She said she came from Crumlin and that her name was Ann.
She told me, 'You can walk me home.' I said, 'I've got a van!'
We turned into a lay-by, where she told me she loved me.
So I gave her my debenture – Block A, Row 3.

That night I met her mother. (She was waiting for us there.)
Stockings round her ankles and curlers in her hair.
She was waiting on the doorstep, and she waved her fist at me.
So I showed her my debenture – Block A, Row 3.

That night when I was sleeping my love proved false to me;
And she left me for another who's known as J.B.G.
I know I'll not forget her for she was the rue of me;
And she's got my debenture – Block A, Row 3.

So take my warning all you lads, for girls the likes of she.
They only want you for one thing – your debenture in Row 3!
So should you go to Crumlin, pray tread the night with care:
Take heed I pray and stay away from that girl with the long
  black hair.

I AM AN ENTERTAINER

'I Am an Entertainer' was written following the Welsh defeat at Twickenham in 1974. The referee that day; a Mr John West, an Irishman, disallowed a perfectly good try (in my opinion) by J. J.Williams and Wales were defeated. I had often wondered since writing the poem what Mr West had thought of it, so when I was introduced to him at a dinner I asked him. 'You've given me a sort of immortality,' he said, 'but I think it's of a rather dubious kind.' He was a lovely man and he had taken the song in the spirit in which it was meant.

Two years later I was having a quiet drink with some friends in the bar of Glynneath Rugby Club on the eve of the Wales–Ireland international at Cardiff. Suddenly the door burst open and four Irish referees burst in with clenched fists shouting, 'Where is he?Where is he?' The bar fell quiet, even some of my best friends moved away from me and pretended they were at another table.

I slowly got up in that hushed room and said quietly, 'Here I am.'

The four wild Irishmen looked across and said, 'Ah, there you are, what are you having to drink?' They had come over for the match and had come down to see Glynneath to invite me to speak at some Referee's Society dinner in Ireland. Unfortunately, I was unable to go, but I shall never forget that night in the rugby club singing a mixture of Irish and Welsh songs in the bar until the early hours and ending up with 'I Am an Entertainer'.

I am an entertainer and I sing for charity;
For Oxfam and for Shelter, for those worse off than me.
Bangladesh, Barnardo's Homes. And though I don't get paid,
It does one good to do some work for things like Christian Aid.

But of all the concerts that I've done for the homeless overseas,
The one I did that pleased me most was not for refugees.
'Twas for a home in Ireland that stands amongst the trees:
The sunshine home in Dublin for blind Irish referees!

THE NORTH ENCLOSURE SONG

I have always thought it a shame that the North Enclosure was done away with at Cardiff Arms Park. Traditionally it was where the singing always started in international matches. It was there that the greatest hwyl* *and atmosphere were always to be found. However, for financial reasons and because of the need for greater crowd control, plastic bucket seating has been installed where for years we had stood in all weathers lashed by wind and rain:*

There were times I couldn't see
But it was the only place to be …

Oh! I'll sing a fond farewell, and a story I will tell
Of when with my little North Enclosure I was there
And I think it's such a shame, it'll never be the same
As when with my little North Enclosure – I was there.

CHORUS
I was there
I was there
With my little North Enclosure I was there

There are stories I can tell, of when I didn't feel too well
But with my little North Enclosure I was there
When there was nowhere I could go and I couldn't wait no more
But with my little North Enclosure I was there.

Oh, I've stood out in the rain and I'd do it all again
With my little North Enclosure I was there
It was there I learnt to sing – 'cos I couldn't see a thing
But with my little North Enclosure I was there.

When the ones that had it planned were all sitting in the stand
With my little North Enclosure I was there
So I think it's such a shame – it'll never be the same
As when with my little North Enclosure I was there.

---

* *hwyl* = fervour, passion, feeling.

THE DIVINE INTERVENTION

This poem was written some time after it was announced that Phil Bennett had been omitted from the Welsh Squad for the game against England at Twickenham in 1976. The decision to omit Bennett caused a great deal of controversy in Wales. People in his home town of Llanelli were throwing themselves in the canals. I wasn't particularly concerned until I realised some of them had tickets on them. So there I was, helping the Red Cross to drag them out – pinching their tickets – and throwing them back in.

Then came the 'Divine Intervention' when both the outside halves named before Phil were injured and, to the great embarrassment of the Welsh selectors, Phil Bennett was asked to play against England after all.

I heard it first on telly I thought that sounded odd
Bevan and Dai Richards in and Phil not in the squad
So I phoned the Rediffusion man when his number I had found
I said, 'The picture's all right, but there's something wrong
    with the sound.'

This chap came round in overalls and told me not to fret
He'd change the speaker and the valve and overhaul the set
He'd finished it by Sunday and left me with a laugh
I switched it on, and the fault had gone
It said, 'Bennett, outside-half.'

Whilst down there in Llanelli the old folk knowing nod
And say recalling Bennett was true an act of God
And a preacher down in Felinfoel spoke in thanks and praise
'The Lord,' he said, 'doth often work in strange and wondrous
    ways.'

And he was there at 'Twickers' round collared in the throng
And he knew full well that Wales would win and he raised his
    voice in song
But I spared a thought for England and for their hopes and pride
It wasn't really fair to them with God on our side.

But this 'frightfully pucker' English chap thought otherwise –
And he knelt in prayer as well
And asked, 'Oh Lord, let us see a try, we're losing I can tell,
Oh Lord, let us see a try, something absolutely twiffic.'
And then J.P.R. scored again and God said, 'You should have
    been specific.'

DAI MORRIS

When David Morris played for the combined Neath and Aberavon side that lost 43–4 to New Zealand in 1973 I wrote:

They didn't leave the score up long
We chipped in for a wreath
Neath blamed Aberavon
And Aberavon, Neath
Some there blamed the linesman
Some blamed you and I
We all blamed the committee
But no one there blamed Dai.

I have always thought it was a great shame that he was never selected for the British Lions. Although he was forced to retire from the international scene with a knee injury it is typical of David Morris that he is as enthusiastic as ever; he is still enjoying his rugby with the village side Rhigos. Perhaps there have been more famous players, but none that are more respected than this gentle man of rugby who's known to all as 'Dai': a shy, unassuming person who gave his everything at all times, asking for nothing in return. He is one of the most genuine people I have ever met, which is why I admire him more than any other player I know.

Now Dai works down at Tower
In a pit called number four,
Some say he was quarried
From a rock a mile below,
He goes to work each morning
Much the same as you or I,
The foreman calls him Mister
But the children call him Dai
Some say that Dai was much too small

This man who works with iron
And that's the reason why they say
He was never made a Lion
And though they never picked him
'*Na fe bois, Felne mae*'*
There's none that's played
Though light he weighed
More genuine than Dai.

* That's how it goes.

E.N.G.L.A.N.D

'E.N.G.L.A.N.D' is a parody on the song 'D.I.V.O.R.C.E', in which a divorcing couple spell out the words they don't want their child to hear or understand.

Our little boy was five years old and quite a little man
And we spelled out all the hurting words so he couldn't understand
Like D.I.V.O.R.C.E and R.E.V.E.N.U.E (H.M)
But the word we're hiding from him now
Tears the heart right out of me

CHORUS
E.N.G.L.A.N.D, we lost to them today
Me and little J. P. R., we cried when we walked away
When we left H.Q, well I think he knew that I had P.M.T*
'Cos it breaks my heart to lose to E.N.G.L.A.N.D

Our little boy is seven by now and I'm an O.A.P
And he thinks that his father's an O.L.D.F.A.R.T
Yes, we spell out all the hurting words and turn our heads to speak
But I can't spell away the hurt and the tears run down my cheek

E.N.G.L.A.N.D, we lost to them today
Me and little J. P. R., we cried when we walked away
When we left H.Q, well I think he knew that I had P.M.T
'Cos it breaks my heart to lose to E.N.G.L.A.N.D
We couldn't even blame the R.E.F.E.R.E.E

---

* Post-match trauma.

THE INCREDIBLE PLAN

Anyone who has tried to get a ticket for a rugby international at Cardiff knows how difficult it is. My Uncle Will, however, got into the ground without a ticket, dressed as one of the St Albans Band (the band that play at Cardiff Arms Park prior to the internationals).

The trouble was all Will's friends and family got to hear of it ('cos he told Florrie Thomas not to tell anybody), and when the next international was due to be played at Cardiff they all wanted to go as well.

'The Incredible Plan' is the story of what happened.

There's a story that's told in the Valleys
And I'll tell it as best as I can
The story of one Will 'McGongale' Morgan
And of his 'Incredible Plan'.
It all started off on a cold winter's night
A night that was strangely so still
When the Rugby Club's General Committee
Banned 'Sine Die' their ticket Sec, my Uncle Will.
(Mind you, he was in the wrong, we knew all along)
There was no point in petitions or pickets
He was caught with this woman at the back of the stand
With the Club's allocation of tickets.
And what made it worse, she wasn't the first
He'd been caught with Ben Walters' wife Ethel
We all knew her with her fox and her fur
She used to wear on Sundays to Bethel.
Anyway, Will was banned 'Sine Die' – he broke down and cried.
I've never seen a man in such sorrow
'Cos like Judas of old he'd sold more than gold
With the Scotland and Wales game tomorrow.
Then he had this idea: he'd go in disguise.

He had it all drawn up and planned.
And he went to the game (to his family's shame)
As one of the St Albans Band.
Back in the village they all got to know
'Make one for me' they'd all say
There was such a demand, it got a bit out of hand
He was making about fifty a day.
So he put an ad, in the *Guardian*
To employ a few men starting Monday
And he did, he started some men – I think about ten,
On three shifts, and some working Sunday.
They made about three or four hundred
When the night shift were sent two till ten.
The jigs were all changed, the tools rearranged,
And they started on ambulance men!
Then they ran out of buttons and bandage –
And policemen were next on the plans.
Whilst 'B' Shift made refs with dark glasses,
Alsatians, white sticks and tin cans!
Then production was brought to a standstill
And the Union could quite understand

When management tabled the motion:
'Things are getting a bit out of hand'.
I'll never forget the day of the match,
The likes of I'll ne'er see again.
I can see them all still coming over the hill:
Hundreds and thousands of men!
The refs came in four double-deckers;
It was going exactly to plan.
And the St Albans Band came in lorries
And the police in a Griff Fender van!
No, I'll never forget that day of the match,
The likes of I'll ne'er see again,
When Queen Street was full of Alsatians
And the pubs full of ambulance men!
It was then I saw Will for the first time:
I was standing on the steps by the 'Grand'.
He was in a camel-hair coat (dressed up as a goat)
Marching in front of the Band!
It was then that the accident happened –

The roads were all slippy and wet.
He was knocked down by a man in a greengrocer's van
And they took him to Davies the Vet.
Now Davies the Vet is a bit short-sighted:
He said, 'I'm afraid it's his heart.
But he wouldn't have lived longer, even if he'd been stronger:
His eyes are too far apart!'
The funeral was held on a Monday
(The biggest I'd ever seen).
The wreaths came in four double-deckers,
And there was one from Prince Charles and the Queen.
(Sorry, from the 'Prince of Wales' and the 'Queens'!)
There were sprays from three thousand policemen,
And one from the St Albans Band.
And the bearers were refs with Alsatians,
Dark glasses, white sticks and tin cans.
We sang at the graveside the old funeral hymns,
And we all went to comfort his son.
What made him sad, he said, was that, 'Dad
Had died not knowing we'd won!'
I couldn't sleep for most of that night,
I kept thinking of what he had said:
'Dad had died not knowing we'd won',
So I dressed when I got out of bed.
And I walked again to that hillside
To that last resting place on a hill.
It was all quiet save when I leant over the grave
And I shouted, 'We hammered them, Will!!!'
And that story is told in the valleys;
I've told it as best as I can.
The legend of one William 'McGonagle' Morgan,
And of his *Incredible Plan*!

WHEN A TEAR FELL FROM GRAHAM HENRY'S EYE

In a far-off foreign field
In a green and pleasant land
Where Wembley's famous towers twin the sky
I knelt in silent grace
When they took me to the place
Where the tear fell from Graham Henry's eye

When a tear fell from Graham Henry's eye
On a day that I'll remember till I die
And we'll place a stone one day
And some words will simply say
Where a Tear Fell from Graham Henry's Eye

On the day it came to pass
On that hallowed Wembley grass
When a single morning star lit up the sky
And now pilgrims travel far
Led by that shining star
To where a tear fell from Graham Henry's eye

Now I know it can't be proved
But he's had his tear ducts removed
So no one thought we'd ever see him cry
But a tear so divine
Fell like water turned to wine
When a tear fell from Graham Henry's eye

Now a man, he took his wife
Who'd been crippled all her life
He laid her on the ground and heaved a sigh
He said, 'I've got to rest a while
I've carried her from Pyle
To where a tear fell from Graham Henry's eye'

Well he laid her gently there
With such a tender loving care
And I swear to God, I'm telling you no lie
That she rose and walked away
For the place on which she lay
Was where a tear fell from Graham Henry's eye

When a tear fell from Graham Henry's eye
On a day that I'll remember till I die
And we'll place a stone one day
And some words will simply say
Where the Tear Fell from Graham Henry's Eye

And the sound of empty chariots filled the sky

THE OUTSIDE-HALF FACTORY

I'll tell you all a story, 'tis a strange and a weird tale:
Of a factory in my valley, not fed by road or rail.
It's built beneath the mountain, beneath the coal and clay.
It's where we make the outside halves that'll play for Wales
    one day.

Down by the council houses, where on a quiet day
You can hear the giant engines digging up the clay.
No naked lights or matches where the raw material's found
In the four-foot seams of outside halves, two miles below the
    ground.

We've camouflaged the mouth with stones, from Bradford
    Northern spies:
From Wigan and from Warrington with promise in their eyes.
And we've boarded up the entrance for the way must not be
    shown;
And we'll tell them all to **** off and make their ******* own!

My dad works down in arms and legs where production's
    running high.
It's he that checks the wooden moulds and stacks them forty high,
But he's had some rejects lately, 'cos there's such a big demand;
So he sells them to the northern clubs, and stamps them
    'second-hand'.

It's there where Harry Dampers works, it's where the money's
    best,
But now his health is failing and the dust lies on his chest.
But he'll get his compensation though his health's gone off
    the rails
When he sees that finished product score the winning try for
    Wales.

But now the belts are empty, came a sadness with the dawn.
And the body-press is idle, and the valley's blinds are drawn.
Disaster struck this morning when a fitter's mate named Ron
Cracked the mould of solid gold that once made Barry John.

Old Harry Dampers (struck with grief), received the final call.
And old Harry has been taken to the greatest outside-half of
    all.
Whose hands are kind and gentle, though they bear the mark
    of nails,
So Harry stamped him 'Number Ten', 'cos he was made in Wales.

And the wheels will go on turning, and trams will run on rails,
To that factory 'neath the mountain making outside-halves for
    Wales.

9-3

Anyone who was at Stradey Park, Llanelli, on that damp October day in 1972, when Llanelli defeated New Zealand's mighty All Blacks by nine points to three will surely never forget the incredible atmosphere at the ground or indeed the scenes that followed that historic win by the 'Scarlets',

And when I'm old and my hair turns grey
And they put me in a chair
I'll tell my great-grandchildren
That their *Datcu** was there.

It was on a dark and dismal day
In a week that had seen rain,
When all roads led to Stradey Park
With the All Blacks here again.
They poured down from the valleys,
They came from far and wide;
There were twenty thousand in the ground
And me and Dai outside!

The shops were closed like Sunday,
And the streets were silent still.
And those who chose to stay away
Were either dead or ill.
But those who went to Stradey, boys,
Will remember till they die
How New Zealand were defeated,

---

* Grandfather.

And how the pubs ran dry.
Oh, the beer flowed at Stradey
(Piped down from Felinfoel),
And the hands that held the glasses high
Were strong from steel and coal.
And the air was filled with singing,
And I saw a grown man cry.
Not because we'd won
But because the pubs ran dry!

Then dawned the morning after
On empty factories.
But we were still at Stradey –
Bloodshot absentees.
But we all had doctors' papers
And they all said just the same:
That we all had 'Scarlet Fever',
And we caught it at the game!

Now all the little babies
In Llanelli from now on
Will be christened Ray or Carwyn,
Derek, Delme, Phil or John.
And in a hundred years again
They'll sing this song for me
Of when the scoreboard read 'Llanelli 9,
Seland Newydd 3'.

And when I'm old and my hair turns grey,
And they put me in a chair,
I'll tell my great-grandchildren
That their *Datcu* was there.
And they'll ask to hear the story
Of that damp October day,
When I went down to Stradey
And I saw the 'Scarlets' play.

A PROP NAMED SIAN

My daddy went north when I was three
When he signed for Wigan for a record fee
When a league scout saw him play at Abercarn
I don't blame him for what he did
I mean they paid him fifteen thousand quid
But before he left he went and named me Sian

Well he must have thought it was quite a joke
And it gotta lot of laughs from a lot of folk
And I grew to hate the thought of my old man
I don't suppose folk would have laughed
If I'd have been an outside-half
But I tell you, life ain't easy as a prop named Sian

But I grew up quick and I grew up keen
And I got picked for the first fifteen
And I roamed the valley towns to hide my shame
And I made me a vow in the local pub
I'd search around each northern club
And find that man that gave me that silly name

Well it was Warrington in mid-July
I just hit town with my butty Dai
We went searching round the clubs for my old man
And in the bar of a Berni Inn at a corner table drinking gin
Sat that dirty dog that named me Sian

I knew at once it was my dad
From an old *Western Mail* that my mother had
And the blue scar on his cheek and his evil eye
I looked at him and I thought, 'Duw, Duw
He's bigger than I thought' but I'd had a few
And I said, 'My name's Sian and this is Dai'

Well Dai hit him right between the eyes
But he got up to Dai's surprise
Pulled out a knife and cut off a piece of Dai's ear
(I said, 'You all right, Dai?' and Dai said, 'What?')

Yea, my dad fought hard and he fought cruel
He played three times for Pontypool
But I could see that he was losing all awhile
He looked at me and he spat and cursed
He went for his gun but I drew mine first
He looked at me and then I saw him smile

He said, 'Son, you just fought one hell of a fight
You can shoot me now, you've got the right
To kill me now and you won't be to blame
But thank me that you're as hard as nails
And come the day you'll play for Wales
You'll thank me for giving you that silly name

'You see, son, Welsh rugby's rough
And if a man's going to make it, he's got to be tough
And I knew I wouldn't be there to help you along
So I named you Sian and I said *ffarwel*
I knew you'd have to get tough and well
It's that name that's helped to make you strong'
(Well, what could I do?)

I got all choked up, threw down my gun
I called him Pa and he called me son
And I went away quite proud of my old man
And I think of him now and again
Every time that I play, every time that we win
And if ever I have a son
I'm going to call him . . . Dylan or Shane, anything but Sian

I WANDERED LONELY

Any Welsh rugby supporter who has been without a ticket on the morning of a Welsh rugby international at Cardiff will understand fully the sentiments expressed in the poem.

I wandered lonely through the crowd
With tired and aching feet.
Ticketless, and down in heart
Where ere I chanced to meet
A man with kindness in his eyes
Who said, 'I got a spare.'
I thanked him there down on my knees
And I asked him, 'But from where?'

He told me then the saddest tale
Of how his wife and he
Were two debenture holders
(North Stand, Block A, Row D).
But since his wife's dear mother died
Oh, she hasn't been the same
And she doesn't feel like going now.
(And I thought, 'What a shame!')

So then I asked, 'But why pick on me?
Don't the family want to go?'
He said, 'They do, but the kick off's at three
And the funeral's ten to four!'

THE DAY GARETH WAS DROPPED

It was the day of the England–Wales rugby international in 1978 at Twickenham. A Welsh supporter who was without a ticket was standing outside the ground in the pouring rain. He called up to some English supporters inside the ground, 'What's happening? What's happening?' and was ungraciously told that all the Welsh team with the exception of Gareth Edwards had been carried off injured.

Some five minutes later there came a great roar from the crowd and the Welsh supporter called out again, 'What happened, what happened, Gareth scored, has he?'

This next poem inspired by the same blinding faith was written at the time when Gareth, seemingly like good wine, was improving with age.

A man came home off afternoons and found his child in woe
And asked him, 'What's the matter *bach*, pray tell what ails you so
Your little eyes are swollen red, your hands are white and shaking.'
'Oh! Dad,' he said, 'I've got bad news, my little heart is breaking
Gareth Edwards has been dropped, 'twas on the news just now
The Welsh selectors must be mad, there's bound to be a row.'
His father said, 'Now, dry your eyes and don't get in a state
Let's be fair mun after all – the man is seventy-eight!'

I WEAR THE CLOTH
OF PARTING WAYS
(EULOGY TO CLIFF MORGAN)

When I was growing up in Glynneath in West Glamorgan, rugby football was a way of life and an integral part of the social fabric of the village.

My first remembered hero was Cliff Morgan CVO from Trebanog in the Rhondda Valley.

He was the epitome of the traditional Welsh outside-half . . . Diminutive, mercurial and inventive. Someone who played with instinct and with joy.

He ran . . . as if the chain had come off his bike . . . !

He became, through sheer personality, Head of Outside Broadcasting at the BBC and became a much respected and loved broadcaster.

It broke his heart when he suffered cancer of the vocal chords, which led to his voice box being removed.

He was to become a dear friend. He even compered some of my concerts in South Africa, where he was rightly revered.

I remember interviewing Cliff in 2013 at his new home in London and I asked him why was he picked for the British Lions Tour of South Africa in 1955, when he was only third-choice outside-half in Wales . . .

He said, 'Because I could play the piano.' On the long flight (in those days) to South Africa he taught his Lions teammates the much-loved South African folk song, 'Sarie Marais'.

> Bring me back to the old Transvaal
> That's where I long to be
> Where yonder amongst the mealies
> By the green thorny trees
> Sarie is waiting for me

Cliff had arranged for a piano to be waiting on the tarmac of the airport, and when the plane landed, the Lions gathered around the piano, resplendent in their tour blazers and ties and, led by Cliff, they sang 'Sarie Marais' . . . 'Bring me back to the old Transvaal.'

That night, the headlines in the Joburg evening paper read,

SURELY THIS IS THE FINEST BRITISH AND IRISH LIONS SIDE EVER TO VISIT SOUTH AFRICA

In that one small gesture he had won over the hearts and minds of the people . . .

When he died after a long illness fought with bravery and dignity, I was deeply honoured to be asked by his family to read an eulogy in the church.

The funeral, in Bainbridge on the Isle of Wight, was deeply moving, with the London Welsh Male Voice Choir resplendent in their red blazers singing 'Bring Him Home' from Les Misérables.

I stood beside Cliff's coffin and read . . . my tribute to Cliff, 'I Wear the Cloth of Parting Ways'.

I wear the cloth of parting ways
For your time with us is done
But you I know would bid us laugh
Just as we've always done
So turn the face of sadness
And the time for tears will pass
As we remember all you were
And fill the parting glass

In the village of Trebanog with its Union Flags unfurled
In a valley where they emptied all the hills to warm the world
Where miners robbed of daylight, would set their pigeons free
Where you carved your name in the wood of the desk
Like a heart carved on a tree

No dingle-starry nights for you, no heron-priested shore
The ribboned coat of your season's fame
Were the scars your father wore
But here you found your heart could sing
What 'ere the eye could see
And sing about the beauty lost and the beauty yet to be

'Twas there you learned to colour words and sing the Psalms
    of Joy
'Twas there an outside-half was born
Within the dreaming boy
But I wear the cloth of parting ways
For loss is such a sorrow
So fill to me 'The Parting Glass'
To brave a new tomorrow

When I will ask of learned men
When days and nights are long
What rhyme or reason could there be
To still a blackbird's song

And so farewell to you, my friend
You're leaving such a wrench
And I'll forgive the countless times
You kept us on the bench

So I wear the cloth of parting ways
For your time with us is done
But you . . . I know would bid us laugh
Just as we've always done
So turn the face of sadness
And the time for tears will pass
As we remember *all* you were
And fill 'The Parting Glass' . . .

THE DEVIL'S MARKING ME

I had a dream the other night,
The strangest dream of all,
I dreamt I was in Heaven,
Away from life's hard call.
It was as I'd imagined,
Where peace ruled all serene.
The signs to Heaven were all in Welsh;
Hell's signs were painted green!

    Painted green, painted green.
    The signs to Heaven were all in Welsh;
    Hell's signs were painted green.

I entered through the heavenly gate,
I heard the heavenly band,
And there was John the Baptist,
On Barry John's right hand!
He plays for the Heaven Welsh XV,
They're very fit and keen.
We'd play the Heaven English
If they could only raise a team!

    Raise a team, raise a team,
    We'd play the Heaven English
    If they could raise a team.

There was Rugby every morning
On a field of golden corn,
And the referee was Gabriel
And he blew on a silver horn.
They tell me we play Hell next week
In the annual charity,
I wouldn't mind but I've been told
The devil's marking me!

    Marking me, marking me,
    I wouldn't mind but I've been told
    The devil's marking me.

But now my dream has faded
And I wake up to the morn,
I find beneath my pillow
A sheaf of golden corn.
So I know that when I go there,
Beyond death's victory,
I'll take my Rugby jersey
On that Gospel train with me.

    Train with me, train with me,
    I'll take my Rugby jersey
    On that Gospel train with me.

THE HALFPENNY PIECE

Now the Mint at Llantrisant are about to reveal
A story the press will release
They'll mint and they'll issue a special new coin
And they'll call it the Halfpenny Piece
I've seen all the drawings and all the designs
But the scale of it . . . took me aback
There's a photo of Halfpenny's face on the front
And Owain Glyndŵr on the back

CHORUS
Oh, they're making a halfpenny piece
They're making a halfpenny piece
It's a story the press are about to release
They say that its value can only increase
The Mint is now guarded by the South Wales Police
Whilst they're making the Halfpenny Piece

We went to Snowdonia to the old Clogau mine
Where the mountains there still bear the scars
And like the miners of old, we'll search for the Gold
That was gifted to us from the stars
The mine will re-open, we'll take on some men
And the value of Gold will increase
And we'll search in the streams and the derelict seams
For Gold for the Halfpenny Piece

The Gold in those mountains is so hard to find
For the seams there are still worked by hand
And the need will increase for the Halfpenny Piece
And they can't keep up with demand
The dust is so pure and precious and rare
And it hides in the quartz and the clay
But the light from my lamp in the dust and the damp
Gave the Clogau's last secret away

There's a piece in the paper, I read it today
The face on the twenty-pound note
You could put a name forward like the late Princess Di
And the governing body would vote
There's been nominations like Churchill of course
Who led us in war and in peace
But still greater to me is the portrait of Leigh
On the face of the Halfpenny Piece

I went to the dentist in Cardiff today
I was nervous, afraid and unsure
And what made it worse was the sight of this nurse
Tying string to the knob of the door
They took out three fillings and the Gold in my crown
I think she'd been trained as a vet
But they later explained as I lay there in pain
'We need all the Gold we can get . . .'

THE GLORY THAT WAS ROME OR: THE GREEN, GREEN GRASS OF ROME

(Sung to the Tune of 'Green, Green Grass of Home')

Well Rome still looks the same, as I stepped down from the plane
And there to meet me was the Pope . . . the Holy Papa . . .
And he told the boys he was glad to see them
Took them on a tour of the Colosseum
Oh! It's good to see the glory that was Rome

CHORUS
Yes, we'll all come to hear the story
Singing, '*Calon lân yn llawn daioni*'
Oh! It's good to see the glory that was Rome

When we reached St Peter's Square, there were thousands
    gathered there
And we waited for the Holy Father's blessing
And he prayed there for the simple reason
They hadn't won a game all season
Oh! It's good to see the glory that was Rome

Then as I wake and look around me as the eternal walls of
    Rome surround me
I wondered how they built the Colosseum
With those great big stones and curving archways
'Cos there were no B&Qs around in those days
Oh! It's good to see the glory that was Rome

I bought some souvenirs, some coins and Roman spears
And a 'paint-by-numbers' Sistine Chapel ceiling
And I bought some cold Peroni beers
And a bottle of the Virgin Mary's tears
Oh! It's good to see the glory that was Rome

Near Flaminio's little ground, an Irish bar we found
And I worried with the bar bill slowly mounting
Till I saw the boys there slyly counting
All the coins they'd nicked from the Trevi Fountain
Oh! It's good to see the glory that was Rome

Our flight back home's delayed, the Pope was so dismayed
He was on our flight and he looked so disappointed
He said, 'We could be here till Monday
And they want me on *Scrum V* on Sunday'
Oh! It's good to see the glory that was Rome

Yes, we'll all come to hear the story
Singing, '*Calon lân yn llawn daioni*'
Oh! It's good to see the glory that was Rome

THE PONTYPOOL FRONT ROW

This song was written as a tribute to the 'Pontypool Front Row' — Charlie Faulkner, Bobby Windsor and Graham Price — who, as well as playing for their club, Pontypool, went on to play with great success for Wales and the British Lions.

Now I'll tell you all a story
About some lads I know.
Who're known throughout the valleys
As the Pontypool Front Row.
It's got a little chorus
And that chorus you all know.
So tell me are you ready?
Up-and-under here we go!

CHORUS
Up-and-under, here we go.
Are you ready, yes or no?
Up-and-under here we go:
It's the song of the Pontypool Front Row.

Now they made a film in London,
It was censored double-X.
The sort of film that frightens one,
Not one of lust and sex.
Mary Whitehouse saw it
And now they'll never show
A film called *Up-and-Under*
Starring the Pontypool Front Row!

We had trouble in Uganda
With President Amin.
So they sent an envoy out there
With a message from the Queen.
To stay that execution
But Amin answered 'No!'
Till a card was sent from the Viet Gwent —
The Pontypool Front Row!

They've had trouble on the railways
With some of soccer's fans.
I've seen them on the terraces
Throwing stones and cans.
They've stopped the soccer specials;
It's a waste of time I know,
'Cos in the end they'll have to send
For the Pontypool Front Row!

There's a programme on the telly,
I watch it when I can,
The story of an astronaut,
The first bionic man.
He cost six-million dollars,
That's a lot of bread I know,
But Wigan offered more than that
For the Pontypool Front Row!

I SAID HE'LL NEVER DO IT

This poem was written after watching Paul Thorburns' incredible seventy-yard (70 yards 8½ inches, or 64.2 metres, to be exact) penalty goal against Scotland in 1986 at Cardiff Arms Park.

I said, 'He'll never do it,' and so did all the boys
'Cos I thought the wind behind had dropped,
And there was a lot of noise.
But I saw him place that tilting ball and start his curving run
And I swear that Thorburn's mighty kick, it passed between
    earth and sun
A darkness fell on Cowbridge
Where they feared for mankind
As prophecies of doomsday came flooding through the mind
'Well, if it is,' the vicar said searching for his text
'According to the Bible, it's boils and locusts next'
But then the shadows came to pass and the light, again it shone
And Thorburn's kick went on, and on, and on, and on, and on.

I watched it Newton's Law defy
And one thing worried me
Would they ever find it if it splashed down in the sea
Or would it, on re-entry, end up burnt and pitted
Or did the makers of the ball have special heat shields fitted?

Someone phoned up NASA, who said, 'It's kind of weird
We had it there right on the screen
And now it's disappeared.'

But there are those who come from Neath
Who didn't find it strange
To everyone but Paul
They said, 'That kick was out of range!'

Mind you, he didn't do it on his own, though I'll give the boy
    his due
The boys up in the West Stand sucked
And the rest of us, we blew.

And then there were the linesmen who squinted to the sky
And heeded careful judgement 'fore they raised their flags on
    high.
And if they judged that kick again
I fear now, alas, they'd have to watch that ball in flight
Through a piece of smoked-up glass

And as the years will come to pass and as the wind behind gets
    stronger
Thorburn's mighty kick, I know, will surely get longer!

And when my children ask me, I'll tell them how it went
The posts were in Glamorgan and he placed the ball in Gwent.

THE SCOTTISH TRIP

'The Scottish Trip' was written on a bus going to Scotland on the Tuesday morning for the Scotland–Wales rugby international when …

We all had doctors' papers
Not one of us in pain
And Harry Morgan buried
His grannie once again

Because of the suspicions aroused over the legality of some illnesses our local GP has refused doctors' papers during the international rugby season. He's now issuing MOT certificates instead: **M***urrayfield* **O***r* **T***wickenham. It didn't happen as the song suggests but it could have … and almost did!*

Oh, we went up to the Hielands of Scotland,
To the land of the loch and the glen.
And we'll all bring our wives back a present
So we can go next time again!

CHORUS
Too-ral-ay, oo-ral-ay, addy,
We went up by train and by car.
When the juice of the barley starts flowing
We all saw the game in the bar.

Oh we loaded the bus up with flagons,
And we left about twenty past seven.
We stopped fourteen times between Neath and Bridgend:
We were still in Glamorgan at eleven.

On the M5 Will spoke to the driver,
He said, 'Can you no stop this bus for a while?'
He said, 'Man alive, we're on the M5.
You'll have to hang on till Carlisle.'

Old Will he climbed out on the sun-roof
And he stood on the bus in disgrace.
He wasn't to know that that bridge was so low,
But he died with a smile on his face!

He was splattered all over the pavement,
And his leek, it was stuffed down his throat.
And I heard his friend say as they scraped Will away,
'My ticket was inside his coat!'

WITH A WHISTLE IN HIS HAND
(TRIPLE CROWN AT CARDIFF)

This poem, which can be sung to the tune of 'Hymns and Arias' (using the same chorus), was written following Wales's win over England at the Principality Stadium on 27 February 2021.

It was a historic occasion in more ways than one because of COVID restrictions.

There were no crowds, no singing, no choirs or marching bands, all integral to the unique and special atmosphere generated by the passionate crowds at Cardiff, who have played no mean part in Wales's success over the years. A Triple Crown win against England at home is a rare thing and it was such a shame that there was no one there to savour it.

The referee, Pascal Gaüzère, came in for a lot of criticism after the game. Many thought England were hard done by . . . but c'est la vie.

The English came to Cardiff as they've done throughout the years
With the sound of 'Flower of Scotland' still ringing in their ears
Eddie came the night before just to walk around the ground
And the team, they came in buses for their ship had run aground

The sun had got up early and tried to warm the day
And the stadium roof was open so God could watch us play
And it all felt very different without a marching band
And without a male voice choir the songs were second-hand

Cardiff streets were empty like a postcard from the past
And the Brynglas tunnel traffic was moving now at last
No fleets of Edwards coaches, no 'Rugby Special' trains
As all the pubs in Cardiff poured their profits down the drains

And the ground was strangely quiet as we waited for the start
As we watched them sing the anthem together and apart
But the moment I'll remember is when Gareth kicked it dead
And time was changing colour as it slowly turned to red

Wales defeated England in a controversial game
Was it just their discipline or the referee to blame?
I spared a thought for Farrell and felt his hurt and pain
And I wondered would he turn his back if he had his time again

On the last train back to London there was such a long delay
As they cleared all the chariots that were strewn along the way
And I felt for poor Eddie as he left that afternoon
'Cos I think he might be furloughed if they don't start winning soon

Now the council down in Cardiff are hoping to install

A Walk of Fame like Hollywood outside the city hall

And they'll come from all the valleys, from the Rhondda and
from Gwent

To see the hands of heroes cast in Aberthaw cement

There's one of Catherine Zeta beside a pointed star

And one of Richard Burton and one of J. P. R.

And there all carved in marble, though the English want it
banned

Is a statue of a Frenchman with a whistle in his hand

HE PICKED A FINE TIME TO PENALISE WHEEL

(Sung to the Tune of 'Lucille')

If there is one incident in a game that I will always remember, it happened in a game between Wales and New Zealand at Cardiff Arms Park.

Wales were leading with a few minutes to go when Geoff Wheel, the great Swansea and Wales second row forward, was penalised quite unfairly by the referee Roger Quittenton for a lineout offence. Subsequent footage showed that Andy Haden and Frank Oliver, the New Zealand locks, had thrown themselves out of the lineout in the hope of getting a penalty, which they subsequently did. Consequently New Zealand won narrowly.

Andy Haden, a great man, admitted to the incident much later in life, no doubt in a vain attempt to cleanse his soul.

In a bar in Rhiwbina, a girl up from Caerau
On a bar stool she took off her ring
I thought I'd get closer, so I walked on over
And asked, 'Can I buy you a drink?'

She said, 'My name's Mandy, you can buy me a brandy
I'm feeling so lonely and blue
I'm hungry for laughter, you're just what I'm after.'
I said, 'What you're after is what I'm after too.'

Then in the mirror I saw him, and I closely watched him
I thought how he looked out of place
And he came to the woman, who sat there beside me
With the saddest of looks on his face

He said, 'I'm from Blaenau,' where I worked as a miner
For a minute I thought I was dead
Then he started shaking, his big heart was breaking
So I bought him a pint and he said,

CHORUS
He picked a fine time to penalise Wheel
The All Blacks were losing with a minute to go
Now I've seen some cheating
But that takes some beating
And this time the hurting won't heal
He picked a fine time to penalise Wheel

Then he left us there drinking, my heart, it was sinking
And I felt kinda guilty and small
And I thought of that miner, as we walked home to Caerau
I walked without talking at all

She said, 'I feel randy,' I said, 'It's the brandy.'
She must have thought that I'd lost my mind
'Cos I couldn't hold her, 'cos the words that he told her
Kept coming back time after time

He picked a fine time to penalise Wheel
The All Blacks were losing with a minute to go
Now I've seen some cheating
But that takes some beating
And this time the hurting won't heal
He picked a fine time to penalise Wheel

THE UNFORGIVING MOMENT

The Rugby World Cup in New Zealand turned out as many people had predicted, with the host nation narrowly beating France in the final. But no one had predicted that Wales would be the country that was to make the greatest impression. They even flew the Welsh flag at 10 Downing Street.

> At Number 10 our flag was flying
> All thro' the night
> Downing Street were edifying
> All thro' the night
> When Cameron rose to share the glory
> Of Wales's still unfolding story
> I even thought of voting Tory
> All through the night

And so then to the semi-final against France and the unfortunate sending off of young Sam Warburton.

The fact that nearly 70,000 people flocked to the Millennium Stadium that morning, sleep still in their eyes, all to watch the game on a big screen was testimony to the intoxicating fever that had gripped the nation like never before.

The price of admission . . . was the colour red.

Red was the colour that opened the doors and the clicking turnstiles. Red was the colour that allowed you access to all areas. Red was the colour of the backstage pass.

They came from Crymych and Caernarfon, Blackwood, Pyle and Aberavon, from the four green fields of Wales, and they sang with painted faces, all beneath a piece of sky, 'Hymns and Arias' and 'Delila' and 'The Fields of Athenry'.

With their flags unfurled, their colours pinned to the mast, they carried their songs to the stadium like . . . a soldier carries his rifle to war, only for their hopes and dreams to be undone in one unforgiving moment.

A moment that broke the heart of a nation.

The crowd at the stadium, their voices stilled, watched in horror and disbelief at the events unfolding on the other side of the world.

Their dream was about to end. Their time in this sun had passed and was no more.

Their disappointment was real and heart-breaking as they emptied into the still-waking streets of Cardiff.

In one frame of film, Wales's remarkable journey had come to an end.

To Welsh followers, and I suspect many others, that was the defining moment of the World Cup in 2011 and one they will always remember.

When all the bunting in the streets of Auckland has blown away, when the weld on the open top buses has cooled and the dwarves have gone back to Snow White, we will remember what might have been in that one unforgiving moment.

Sometimes, though only rarely, more can be achieved in defeat than victory, and though there were no selfish gains, no ribboned coats of a season's fame, this young Welsh side earned the respect of the rugby-playing world.

There is no denying that New Zealand deserved to win the World Cup after many years in the wilderness, and though black was the colour of the ribbons tied to the Webb Ellis Cup in Auckland . . . red was the price of admission.

WITH A WEE DRAM AND A SONG

'With a Wee Dram and a Song' tells of some of my treasured memories of visiting Scotland for the Scotland–Wales rugby international at Murrayfield and of the welcome we have always received from the Scottish people. It is because of the affinity, kinship and friendship we have that:

> *Some never get to see the game*
> *E'en though we journey long*
> *For they bid us 'Ae Fond Welcome'*
> *With a wee dram and a song.*

Oh! We'll go to the highlands of Scotland and to bonnie Teviot dales
And they'll bid us 'ae fond welcome' for we've journey far from Wales.
And they'll stand with banners waving in kilt and sporraned throng
And bid us 'ae fond welcome' with a wee dram and a song.

CHORUS
With a wee dram and a song
With a wee dram and a song
They'll bid as ae fond welcome
With a wee dram and a song.

Then it's in some chemist on Sunday, your legs they feel like lead

Asking 'Have you got something for . . .' when you haven't been to bed

Then with bleary eyes we'll all swop ties, and the bus driver says, 'C'mon it's ten to ten',

And you've gone and squashed your haggis and lost your mac again.

And we'll check into some small hotel and say, 'We live by Gâr'

And pay for 'Bed & Breakfast' and never leave the bar

And they'll ask us for a wee Welsh song and your eyes are bloodshot red

And your voice has gone but you carry on – when all you want's your bed.

Then you'll drag yourself to Murrayfield and the snow has turned to rain

And you swear there on the terrace you'll never drink again

And the crowd sing 'Flow'r of Scotland' and you're caught up in the sway

And you spend the first ten minutes facing the other way.

And then you remember … you haven't bought a present, and
    you're wondering what to get her
And you're in this M6 Service Station trying to buy a Pringles
    cashmere sweater
But there's only trains and plastic planes and you're searching
    all in vain
You've spent four days in Scotland and bought a doll from Spain.

And then it's home on Sunday and another trip it ends
With a parting gift of heather from my 'ain auld border friends'.
I'll miss a shift on Monday as aye oft times I've done
Then read the Sunday papers to see if Wales have won.

For some never get to see the game e'en though we journey long
For they bid us 'ae fond welcome with a wee dram and a song'
And if we lose it matters not for there the sadness ends
For defeat's ne'er counted as a loss if it be the gain of friends
And may that friendship ever last and may it journey long
To bid us 'ae fond welcome' with a wee dram and a song!

IF

This is a rugby version of 'If', as it would have been read by Rudyard Kipling if his son had been a referee!

If you can keep your head when all about you
    Are losing theirs and blaming it on you
If you can trust yourself when all the crowd doubt you
    And wonder why you blew

If you can wait and not be tired of waiting
    For tempers to subside
    Or being hated – don't give way to hating
    Or favour either side

If you can play advantage and bear the crowd's derision
    And the offer of new glasses as they question each decision

If you can force your heart and nerve and sinew
    To serve your turn when you know your legs have – gone
    And keep up with play and hope and pray
    Some second row will knock on

If you can talk with crowds and keep your virtue
    Or talk with our committee
    And not lose the common touch
    Neither foes or toilet rolls can hurt you
    All our boys are with you – but none *too* much

If you can control that unforgiving minute
    With tempers running high
    With a calmness born of knowing why – you disallowed
      that try

If you can watch the moment all again
    When they show the game that night
    And watch the replay all slowed down
    And admit the crowd were right

Then if you 'ref' that side again
    And you're remembered as '*the one*'
    I'd get escorted from the ground
    If I were you – my son

ALL BENEATH A PIECE OF SKY

In 2005 Wales claimed their first Grand Slam win since 1978 – a wait of twenty-seven years.

I was asked by the Welsh management to write a song and to sing the national anthem with Charlotte Church and Katherine Jenkins . . . a rare privilege.

And they came from Cork and Dublin
All to answer Ireland's call
And I hope their man O'Driscoll
Doesn't get the ball at all
And we sang with painted faces
All beneath a piece of sky
'Hymns and Arias' and 'Delilah'
And 'The Fields of Athenry'

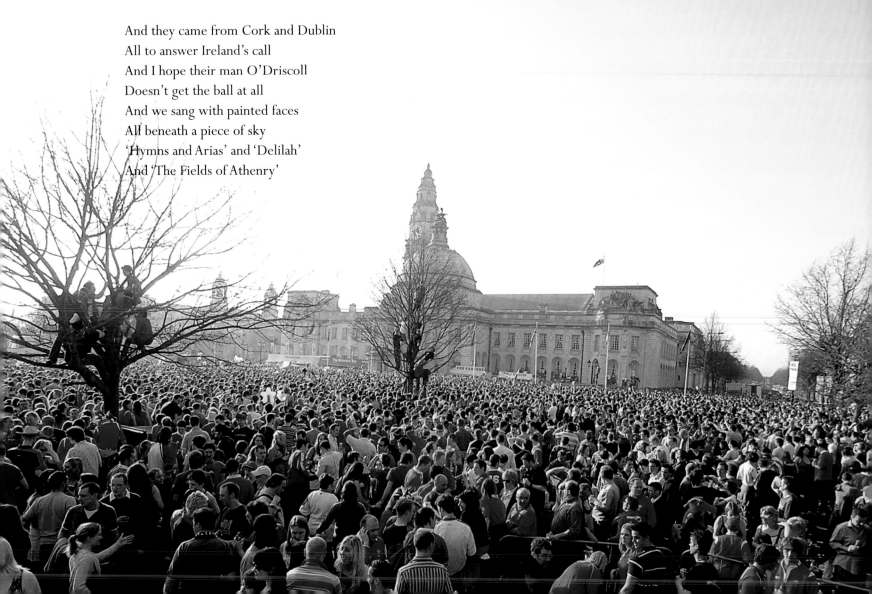

TEN THOUSAND INSTANT CHRISTIANS

One of the great influences on the Welsh way of life has undoubtedly been the tradition of the 'chapels'. It is therefore sad to see their decline and sadder still to see them converted into bingo halls and the like.

I remember one rugby international in which we'd been singing the old Sunday school favourites in the pubs of Cardiff all the morning: 'Rwy'n canu fel cana'r aderyn', 'Draw draw yn China'. Then again at the ground it was Welsh hymns that rang from the terraces: 'Cwm Rhondda' and 'Calon Lân'.

It seemed strangely sad therefore that on the way back from the match we should pass a chapel with a sign outside which said 'FOR SALE'. Seeing that sign influenced me to write this song.

When He sees the Hope & Anchor where we sang before the game,
Where 'Cwm Rhondda' and 'Delilah' first sounded both the same.
The bar was filled with singing, and the songs came on a tray.
And Saturday was Sunday, I wonder what He'll say?

When He sees the North Enclosure with its belly-full of ale,
And sees that male-voice flagon, sing to the twisted barrier-rail.
'Cwm Rhondda' and 'Penmachno' – hymns of yesterday –
But only half remembered, I wonder what He'll say.

When He sees those touch-line tenors, with their copies made of sand:
Ten thousand instant Christians, and the Glynneath Silver Band.
'Come on mun, ref, for Christ's sake, the ball was still in play,'
Ten thousand instant Christians, I wonder what He'll say.

When He sees that empty chapel with its locked and shuttered doors,
And sees that dusty Bible, cobweb-covered floors.
The number slowly dwindling, much fewer now each day:
Calfaria now a bingo hall, I wonder what He'll say.

DID YOU UNDERSTAND?

'Did You Understand?' was a song written during the Miners' Strike of 1972, the first of two strikes which were directly responsible for the defeat of the Conservative Party in the general election that followed.

I remember singing at the time in a village hall in Llanelli. It was a time when the supply of electricity was being rationed to conserve the coal stocks at the power stations. Halfway through the concert the supply to the hall was cut off, leaving us without any means of amplification or lighting.

I sang this song in that hall in complete darkness that night with just an acoustic guitar. I knew from the reaction to the song that the public sympathy in the town of Llanelli lay entirely with the collier at that time.

I remember the time of the collier and the candle,
Of a long bitter fight that darkened the land.
And I asked you the question but you wouldn't answer,
When I asked you the question, did you understand?
Collier laddie, collier boy.

I saw mills and machines, all lying there idle,
A million or more unemployed in the land.
And I asked them the question but they wouldn't answer,
When I asked them the question, did they understand?
Collier laddie, collier boy.

Then I saw the ones sit in the seats of decision;
They sat and they judged the miners' demand.
And they all heard the case of the lowly paid miner,
But though they decided, did they understand?
Collier laddie, collier boy.

Then I saw an old collier, whose body lies broken,
Claimed by the dust much finer than sand.
And I asked him the question, though now he can't answer,
I'll ask him the question and he'll understand.
Collier laddie, collier boy.

A WINTER TOO LATE
(1984-85 MINERS' STRIKE SONG)

Did they come to get the video
And the money that you'd spent
Did you worry about the mortgage
Did you manage with the rent
Did you stop the Sunday papers
Find the time to fix the roof
And did you tell the kids that
You'd cancelled Magaluf

Did you think it all was hopeless
That the fight could not be won
With miner turned on miner
And father turned on son
And sometimes did you wonder
As to who and what was right
In time will you forgive the ones
Who didn't share the fight

Did you raise your voice in anger
At the strong arm of the law
And were you disillusioned
By the bitter scenes you saw
Did you stand at picket duty
At dawn's first waking light
So many lines of policemen pawned
In someone else's fight

Did you get MacGregor's letter
Did you laugh at what it said
Did you listen then to Arthur
Do you think he was misled
Did he lead the miners bravely
Or was he much too vain
Would he call a ballot
If he had the chance again

Did you see the banners waving
And the brass band sounding loud
As the Maerdy men returned to work
Defiant and unbowed
And when the year had passed, lads
Did you wonder was it fate
That brought the bitter weather
A winter just too late

And when the strike was over
Did you stop to count the cost
And wonder what was won, lads
And wonder what was lost
And will you move away now
Has the hope of youth been slain
Or does the hawthorn by the pithead
Still blossom in the rain

And will you move away now
Has the hope of youth been slain
Or does the hawthorn by the pithead
Still blossom in the rain

ABERFAN

I happened once to pass this way where the Iron Masters ruled
But now the pit wheels turn no more and the furnaces have cooled
And high above the valley floor where the Taff Vale railway ran
The spoils of waste and negligence and the legacy of man
And I walked on through Elysian fields with autumn's leaves unfurled
In a valley where they emptied all the hills to warm the world
Where warnings went unheeded and man ignored the call
And just like Crawshay's three-faced clock
Turned faceless to the wall
And I walked through fields of bracken
And watched the day unfold
As the alchemy of autumn turned all the hills to gold
Where on that fateful morning came scenes of such despair
Beyond our understanding a grief beyond compare
When I will ask of learned men when days and nights are long
What rhyme or reason could there be to still the morning song
ALL THINGS BRIGHT AND BEAUTIFUL
All CREATURES GREAT AND SMALL
ALL THINGS . . .
And I will plant a flower there and tie a small balloon
And wonder why in Aberfan did autumn come so soon

COAL PICKING

It was common in the villages of south and north Wales, Yorkshire, Lancashire and the North East to go what is known as 'coal picking'.

The 'spoils' of the seams of the 'Cornish' and 'Yard' were tipped on the hills above the pit villages.

Among the 'spoils' there were 'gems' of coal that shone like 'diamonds' in the bright sunshine.

The women and children of the village would carry hessian bags and sacks or drag prams and trolleys to collect these precious gifts.

My grandfather Jonah, who became my father figure, I called Datcu *or 'cu (the South Walian word for 'grandfather') – which is what my granddaughters Rhosyn Alaw and Evelyn Grace now call me.*

He taught me to approach the 'tips' with the sun low in the sky and behind us. This enabled us to see the coal glinting in the morning sunshine as it 'gave the old mountain's last secret away'.

I remember the time when we went coal picking
On the tips of the mountain, just me and *Datcu*
And our pram wheels were spindled with five o'clock faces
When we went coal picking, me and *Datcu*

We passed the steel ropes that had hauled many journeys
With the dregs of the seams just as old as the sea
And we drank with our hands from the streams of the mountain
When we went coal picking, me and *Datcu*

The cold sun of winter shone bright on that morning
As we climbed the old incline and around the long turn
Where a red-bricked old engine house stood in the clearing
Haunted by nettle and bramble and fern

We broke open stones that the past had kept hidden
That shared the long sleep with a leaf from a tree
That blinked in the light of a born-again morning
When we went coal picking, me and *Datcu*

The climb it got steeper with the pram wheels complaining
And the coal still lay hidden in the dust of its day
Till the sun picked its way through the gorse and the bramble
And gave the old mountain's last secret away

The tips have long gone now and the past has grown over
Like the heart that I carved in the wood of a tree
But the memories remain as fresh as that morning
When we went coal picking, me and *Datcu*

Some weeks ago, when compiling this anthology, a local builder who is a keen archivist of local history sent me a clipping out of a newspaper from 1943. It was the report of a mining explosion at a local colliery in the Dulais Valley, Onllwyn No. 3.

It detailed the admitted neglect of Messrs Evans and Bevan of Neath, the mine owners.

That neglect led to the death of my father a month before I was born.

My mother, only twenty-something at the time, was awarded a meagre £300 to care for her child.

What made painful reading was the statement by mine owners: 'There was an explosion in the Grey seam of Onllwyn No. 3 . . . The damage was not extensive and work resumed shortly after . . .'

'In the dust and the damp of a seam called "The Grey"
There was no great damage, at the end of the day . . .'

ONLLWYN PIT EXPLOSION

FOUR COLLIERS INJURED

An explosion at the Onllwyn No. 3 Pit, Banwen, on Friday of last week resulted in four colliers being badly burned. They are: Irvin John, Heol Merchog, Banwen; Watkin Harvey, Roman Road, Banwen; David Thomas Lewis, Penybach, Abercrave, and Leonard Boyce, Robert Street, Glynneath. All four were removed to the Swansea Hospital.

The colliery, which is owned by Messrs. Evans and Bevan, Neath, was working fully at the time, but the effect of the explosion was confined to the area in which the injured men were working on the Grey seam.

The damage was not extensive, and work was resumed shortly afterwards.

Explosion Sequel

As the result of an explosion at Onllwyn Colliery, Onllwyn, on August 20, 1943, Mary Elizabeth Boyce, aged 30, widow of Leonard Maxwell Boyce, of Robert-street, Glynneath; Watkin Harvey, aged 27, of 10, Roman-road, Banwen; John Irving, aged 40, of 15, Council Houses, Banwen; Trevor Jones, aged 39, Aberaman, Aberdare; and David Thomas Lewis, aged 60, of Penybank, Abercrave, claimed damages from Messrs. Evans and Bevan, colliery proprietors, High-street, Neath, for alleged negligence.

Boyce, it was stated, was fatally injured, and severe burns to three of the other men necessitated their removal to hospital. Lewis was struck on the head and rendered unconscious. The plaintiffs alleged the explosion was due to a breach of statutory duty on the part of defendants in failing to provide proper ventilation at the place where the men were working.

Liability was admitted, and Mr. Justice Croom-Johnson awarded to Mrs. Boyce £1,750, of which £300 was for a year-old child, with £23 funeral expenses and costs.

To Lewis, on account of his age, he awarded £912 with costs. Awards to the other three men were made under various heads, and were left to be calculated and announced to-day.

CLOSE THE COALHOUSE DOOR

When I was just a lad and the coalman's lorry came
I'd run and tell my granddad, 'Hey *Datcu*
Can I help you please, can I get your dungarees
Can I help you, can I please, *Datcu*?'

He told me, 'Ask your mother, better ask your mother first
Perhaps she'll cut a box for you and my jack will quench your thirst
And you can have my shovel the one I've always had
And you can come and help me and be my collier lad'

So I put on my old trousers with a hole ripped in one knee
And I hoped the boys would see me helping my *Datcu*
I helped *Datcu* to make a wall and to make a passing place
And when he wasn't looking I rubbed coal dust in my face

Then I started getting tired, my hands were scratched and sore
'C'mon,' I said, '*Datcu*, c'mon, we don't need any more
Leave those last few lumps,' I said, 'there's only three or four
C'mon,' I said, '*Datcu*, c'mon, let's close the coalhouse door'

He leaned his shovel 'gainst the wall and took me on his knee
And said, 'Now listen here, my lad, and listen well to me
If you had seen where men had been in places low and bad
You wouldn't leave a lump behind, not one, my collier lad'

'But then you're just a collier boy and you're tired, yes, I know
Come, my little collier boy, let's close the coalhouse door
Come, my little collier boy, come, my little collier boy
Come, my little collier boy, let's close the coalhouse door . . .'

DUW! IT'S HARD

'Duw! It's Hard' (God! It's Hard) is a song I wrote after seeing a supermarket advertised in a local newspaper. The supermarket's address was given as 'The Old Pit Head Baths, Ebbw Vale'. The advertisement appeared at the time when many collieries were being closed in south Wales, and it illustrated the changes that were taking place in the mining communities at that time.

The song has always meant a great deal to me, because my father was killed in a colliery explosion and I worked for many years underground myself.

In our little valley they've closed the colliery down,
And the pithead baths is a supermarket now.
Empty journeys red with rust rolled to rest amidst the dust
And the pithead baths is a supermarket now.

CHORUS
'Cos it's hard, Duw it's hard.
It's harder than they will ever know.
And it's they must take the blame
The price of coal's the same,
But the pithead baths is a supermarket now.

They came down here from London because our output's low,
Briefcases full of bank clerks that have never been below.
And they'll close the valley's oldest mine, pretending that
    they're sad.
But don't you worry, Butty *bach*, we're really very glad.

My clean-clothes-locker's empty now, I've thrown away the key
And I've sold my boots and muffler and my lamp-check one-
    five-three.
But I can't forget the times we had, the laughing midst the fear,
'Cos every time I cough I get a mining souvenir.

I took my old helmet home with me, filled it full of earth
And I planted little flowers there, they grew for all they're worth.
And it's hanging in the glass-house now – a living memory,
Reminding me they could have grown in vases over me.

But I know the local magistrate, she's got a job for me
Though it's only counting buttons in the local factory.
We get coffee breaks and coffee breaks, coffee breaks and tea,
And now I know those dusty mines have seen the last of me.

'Cos it's hard, Duw it's hard.
It's harder than they will ever know.
And if ham was underground, would it be twelve bob a pound?
The pithead baths is a supermarket now.
Aye, the pithead baths is a supermarket now.

MINERS' FORTNIGHT
(ODE TO BARRY ISLAND)

When I was a lad, the last week in July and the first week in August were traditionally 'Miners' Fortnight'. The collieries would close, horses were brought blinking to the surface and whole villages would move some twenty or thirty miles down the road to Porthcawl or Barry Island.

These then are some of my childhood recollections.

I remember 'Miners' Fortnight' when I was just a lad
It was always Porthcawl or Barry Island
And the weather always bad
In a brand-new shirt, and shoes that hurt
The ones Mam saved to buy
To go to Barry Island on the last week in July.

We'd catch a bus down by the square –
My bucket in my hand
Then all the fuss to get on the bus
And we always had to stand
Then I'd be sick and my shoes I'd kick
The ones Mam saved to buy
To go to Barry Island on the last week in July.

So they'd put me by the driver for me to have some air
And my mother'd say, 'He's never this way',
And she'd come and comb my hair
Then I'd see the sea and I'd want to pee
If I couldn't I would cry
When I went to Barry Island on the last week in July.

Our caravan 'The Water's Edge' ten miles from the sea
We'd drag the cases over and we didn't have the key
Then, we couldn't light the gas lamp – I've gone and marked my tie
When we went to Barry Island, on the last week in July.

I'm on the beach, it's Sunday, I've met a friend called Russ
I'll have to buy another bucket – I've left mine on the bus
I've cut my foot – it's bleeding, my cousin says, 'You'll die
And they'll bury you in Barry on the last week in July.'

I'm going to the fair tonight, my bucket full of shells
The weather forecast's settled now, with dry and sunny spells
I've bought *Mamgu** a present and waved the sea goodbye
My mother's found my plastic mac and the weather's nice and dry.

Aye that's how I remember Miners' Fortnight
When I was just a lad
Porthcawl or Barry Island, and the weather always bad.

* Grandmother.

THE SIONI WINWNS MAN (THE JOHNNY ONIONS MAN)

The Breton traders, with their pink Roscoff onions, their jaunty berets and handkerchiefs of blue, were once a common sight in the Welsh valleys and towns. They were not allowed to sell their wares until they were sixteen years of age. So many of them who were much younger painted moustaches on their faces to make them look older . . . and they became known as Le Petit Jean, *'The Little Johnnies'* . . .

It's a memory of my childhood
That I can still recall
When I watched old Johnny Onion
Lean his bike against the wall
And he'd 'peddle' all his harvest
That hung down from the bar
And with his bike and beret
He'd wish me *bore da*!

CHORUS
The Johnny Onion Man, throughout the streets
    we ran
To see old Johnny Onion
The *Sioni Winwns* Man

From the sea-washed turf of Roscoff
The farmers long ago
Sprinkled all their onions
With the seaweed from the shore
And they say that age-old secret
That they've used since time began
Was why they tasted sweeter
From the Johnny Onion Man

And then to Cardiff's dockland
Their bikes all laden down
With strings of onion rosé
To sell throughout the town
And they went up to the valleys
Where a legend round them grew
And I miss old Johnny Onion
With his handkerchief of blue

But now we never see them
And I think it's such a shame
For the ones they sell in Tesco's
They just don't taste the same
And I miss old Johnny Onion
The 'Beret' Petit Jean
And the pink and jewelled harvest
Of the Johnny Onion Man

And I wonder where they've gone now
And are they peddling still
And do they push their weary bikes
Along some tired hill
And do they still remember
When they called, '*Bonjour, Maman*'
As they travelled through the valleys
The Johnny Onion Man

WHEN JUST THE TIDE WENT OUT

I wrote this poem at the height of the first lockdown of the COVID pandemic.

Some friends suggested I should share it on social media. I agreed and it went 'viral'.

It was viewed millions of times by people from all over the world and I received hundreds of letters.

I even had one from Kensington Palace asking if I would read the poem to Their Royal Highnesses the Duke and Duchess of Cambridge in the grounds of Cardiff Castle.

They were on a visit to Wales to thank the frontline workers of the NHS for their courage and commitment during unprecedented times.

I was honoured to have been asked and I rewrote some lines that morning to fit the occasion:

> *And when these days are over and memories remain*
> *Of children painting rainbows and the sun shone through the rain*
> *And I remember nurses who stretchered all the pain*
> *Who Kate and William came to thank on the Queen's own Royal train*

Last night as I lay sleeping, when dreams came fast to me
I dreamt I saw Jerusalem beside a tideless sea
And one dream I'll remember as the stars began to fall
Was Banksy painting Alun Wyn on my neighbour's garage wall
And dreams like that sustain me till these darkest times have
   passed
And chase away the shadows no caring night should cast
But times like this can shine a light as hardship often can
To see the best in people and the good there is in man

And I remember Swansea with nobody about
When the shops were closed like Sunday and just the tide
   went out

And I remember Mumbles with the harbour in its keep
And the little boats at anchor that fish the waters deep
And I heard the seabirds calling as the gulls all wheeled about
But all the town was sleeping now and just the tide went out

And when these days are over and memories remain
When children painted rainbows and the sun shone through
   the rain
And I'll remember nurses who stretchered all the pain
And I hope the carers never see a time like this again

And I remember Swansea with nobody about
When the shops were closed like Sunday and just the tide
   went out

And I prayed that time for Boris, when he knocked on Heaven's door
And I thought of voting Tory, which I've never done before
And though the sun is shining now I've no immediate plans
So I'll write a book on 'Staying In' and 'Ways To Wash Your Hands'

And I'm still here in lockdown, more weeks of staying in
I'm running out of vodka now so I've started on the gin
And my neighbours are complaining, I've heard them scream and shout
With the noise the bins are making when I take the empties out

And I remember Swansea with nobody about
When the shops were closed like Sunday and just the tide went out

Some wanted Christmas cancelled but the Piper calls the tune
And 'Hark! The Herald Angels Sing' wouldn't sound the same in June
So I'll wait here for my vaccine though I know there's some delay
And I'll order mine on Amazon and I'll get it yesterday

And when all this is over, and our fragile world survives
I hope that God is caring now for the ones who gave their lives
And I pray we'll find an answer, for my faith is cast in doubt
And God draws back the heavens and all the stars come out

And I'll remember mornings with nobody about
When the shops were closed like Sunday, and just the tide went out

AR LAN Y MÔR (BY THE SEA SHORE)

'Ar Lan y Môr' is a lovely traditional Welsh folk song in which the writer tells of how he used to meet the girl he loved by the sea shore where there were red roses (rhosys cochion) and white lilies (lilis gwynion), and where rosemary and thyme grew amongst the rocks. Some words I once wrote roughly translate the second verse, and, hopefully, convey some of the feeling.

Along the shore we walked together
Where thyme grows wild amongst the heather
'Twas there we whiled away the hours
Where all the rocks are strewn with flowers

In the song he goes on to say that although now the girl he loves is far across the sea, his thoughts are always with her.

Ar lan y môr mae rhosys cochion
Ar lan y môr mae lilis gwynion
Ar lan y môr mae nghariad inne
Yn cysgu'r nos a chodi'r bore

Ar lan y môr mae carreg wastad
Lle bûm yn cyfarfod gynt â'm cariad
Oddeutu hon mae teim yn tyfu
Ac ambell sbrigyn o rosmari

Tros y môr y mae fy nghalon
Tros y môr y mae f'ochneidion
Tros y môr y mae f'anwylyd
Sy'n fy meddwl i bob munud

BUGEILIO'R GWENITH GWYN (WATCHING THE WHITE WHEAT)

William Hopkin (known as 'Will Hopkin' the bard) was born at Llangynwyd in 1700. The tradition of Ann Thomas's hapless love for him ('The Maid of Cefn Ydfa') is widely known in Wales, especially in Glamorganshire. The bard wrote many songs in her honour, but the most popular is 'Bugeilio'r Gwenith Gwyn' – 'Watching the White Wheat' – sung to the melody previously known as 'Yr Hen Gelynen'. It comes from the folk song collection of Miss Jane Williams, Aberpergwm, Glynneath.

Mi sydd fachgen ieuanc ffôl.
Yn byw yn ôl fy ffansi.
Myfi'n bugeilio'r gwenith gwyn,
Ac arall yn ei fedi.
Pam na ddeu di ar fy ôl,
Ryw ddydd ar ôl ei gilydd?
Gwaith r'wy'n dy weld, y feinir fach,
Yn lanach, lanach beunydd!

Glanach glanach wyt bob dydd,
Neu fi sy' â'm ffydd yn ffolach.
Er mwyn y Gŵr a wnaeth dy wedd,
Gwna im drugaredd bellach:
Cwn dy ben gwêl acw draw.
Rho i mi'th law, wen dirion;
Gwaith yn dy fynwes bert ei thro.
Mae allwedd clo fy nghalon!

I rose at dawn's first waking light
And wandered midst the flowers
And longed that you were by my side
In that morning's early hours
To take your hand and walk awhile
And see the new day dawning
And to kiss you gently on your cheek
As dew fresh kissed the morning.

Tra bo dŵr y môr yn hallt,
A thra bo ngwallt yn tyfu
A thra bo calon dan fy mron
Mi fydda'n ffyddlon iti:
Dywed i mi'r gwir heb gêl
A rho dan sêl d'atebion,
P'un ai myfi neu arall Ann
Sydd oreu gan dy galon.

SWANSEA TOWN

(written by John Davis with additional lyrics by Max Boyce)

This lovely song, with its simple lyric and haunting melody, tells of the 'hiraeth' and longing a young man has for Swansea Town, and the happiness he feels in going home.

I'm going home to Swansea Town
The day is nearly dawning.
I'm going home to the seaport sound
One lovely seatown morning.

I'm going home to Swansea Town
To where the ways are brambled.
'Neath the seatown sky where seagulls cry
Where as a boy I rambled.

One day I'll walk this valley
See the lovely golden shore
Let others search the whole world over
I'm going home once more

And she'll be waiting there for me
She'll be glad to see me.
And I'll not leave my town again
A fortune won't persuade me.

I'm going home to Swansea Town
The day is nearly dawning.
I'm going home to the seaport sound
One lovely seatown morning.

HIRAETH

'Hiraeth' is a haunting traditional folk song I have been singing on recent concert tours. I explain there is no single English word that means quite the same (it is a deep longing, more often than not for one's homeland).

The song asks the question of what is hiraeth made that it never rusts with age or sullies with time.

I've written an English verse that I hope conveys the true feeling of this beautiful song.

Tell me then, you men of learning
Why is hiraeth such a yearning
Why when darkness minds to hide me
Hiraeth comes and sleeps beside me

Material possessions, gold, silver, velvet and silk all fade in time, but hiraeth *lasts for ever.*

Dwedwch, fawrion o wybodaeth,
O ba beth y gwaethpwyd hiraeth;
A pha ddefnydd a roed ynddo
Na ddarfyddo wrth ei wisgo.

Derfydd aur a derfydd arian,
Derfydd melfed, derfydd sidan;
Derfydd pob dilledyn helaeth,
Eto er hyn ni dderfydd hiraeth.

Hiraeth mawr a hiraeth creulon,
Hiraeth sydd yn torri 'nghalon,
Pan fwy' dryma'r nos yn cysgu
Fe ddaw hiraeth ac a'm deffry.

Hiraeth, Hiraeth, cilia, cilia,
Paid â phwyso mor drwm arna',
Nesa tipyn at yr erchwyn,
Gad i mi gael cysgu gronyn.

RHONDDA GREY

'The tools are on the bar' is an old mining term used commonly in the south Wales coalfield to signify the end of the shift, when it was time to 'put the tools on the bar'. The bar was a rod of iron on which the collier kept his tools locked for safety.

This mining expression also became symbolic of ill-health. Old colliers taking their grandsons for a walk on Sunday mornings would be forced to stop a while to fight for breath because of 'dust'.

'Wait a minute, bach,' they'd say, 'the tools are on the bar.'

I have used that expression in a song which tells about a colour. A colour not found in the slates or the pavements of the valley towns but only in the faces of old men who worked underground for many years. I've called that colour and the song, 'Rhondda Grey'.

One afternoon from a council school
A boy came home to play.
With paints and coloured pencils
And his homework for the day.
'We've got to paint the valley, Mam,
For Mrs Davies' Art.
What colour is the valley, Mam?
And will you help me start?'

'Shall I paint the Con. Club yellow,
And paint the Welfare blue?
Paint old Mr Davies red
And all his pigeons too?
Paint the man who kept our ball –
Paint him looking sad?
What colour is the valley, Mam?
What colour is it, Dad?'

'Dad, if Mam goes down the shop
To fetch the milk and bread,
Ask her to fetch me back some paint –
Some gold and white and red.
Ask her fetch me back some green,
(The bit I've got's gone hard).
Ask her fetch me back some green;
Ask her, will you, Dad?'

His father took him by the hand
And they walked down Albion Street
Down past the old Rock Incline
To where the council put a seat.
Where old men say at the close of day
'Dy'n ni wedi g'neud ein siar' *
And the colour in their faces says
'The tools are on the bar.
The tools are on the bar.'

---

* We've done our share.

'And that's the colour that we want
That no shop has ever sold.
You can't buy that in Woolies, lad,
With your reds and greens and gold.
It's a colour you can't buy, lad,
No matter what you pay.
But that's the colour that we want:
We call it Rhondda Grey.'

SLOW-MEN AT WORK

If I was to ask who the hardest working men in Britain today are, no doubt some would say, the collier or the trawlerman in icy seas, but in my opinion the hardest working men must be the council roadmen.

I remember one bitterly cold January morning, I happened to pass some council roadmen. Some of them (if not all of them) were leaning on their shovels shivering. I called out, 'Why don't you do some work to keep warm?'

One of them shouted back, 'I'd rather be cold than tired.'

Then there was another occasion when I passed a hole in the road from which I could hear council roadmen singing, 'Happy birthday to you, happy birthday to you.'

I enquired whose birthday it was, and was told, 'It's the hole's; he's one today.'

My favourite council roadman story, however, concerns the foreman who smashed his shovel down on a poor defenceless snail. When he was asked why had he done it, he answered, 'He's been following me all day.'

This song was written in tribute to the men whose shoulders are always to the wheel: the council roadmen. The idea for the song was suggested to me by one of their signs which read 'SLOW — MEN AT WORK'.

There is a band of loyal men
Who come in their lorries but they don't say when.
What they do, well, I just can't say –
They're either coming or they're going away.

CHORUS
And they keep their billy-cans brewing,
They keep their billy-cans brewing.
They keep their billy-cans brewing
And they brew a little more each day!

But it's a dangerous job both cruel and hard;
They risk their lives when the floods are bad.
One drowned last week whilst clutching his spade:
He slipped and he fell in the tea he'd made!

Have you seen them working on the road,
Sweating and toiling with a heavy load?
Seen them working with no thought of tea?
Well, if you have, you don't live by me!

They say that Rome wasn't built in a day,
And there was one big long delay,
The reason was and it's a fact,
The council had the main contract!

IS GOD IN HIS PAINT SHOP

Is God in his paint shop at a loss what to do
His canvas is old but his brushes are new
He'll choose every colour, each shade and each hue
And sometimes I wonder will he run out of blue

He's all sorts of brushes in bottles and jars
And he'll paint all of Heaven and the silvery stars
And he'll paint the day dawning with fresh falling dew
And sometimes I wonder will he run out of blue

The spring he's fresh painted where the winter has been
And time changes colour when it's twenty to green
He's red for the sunset when the day slips from sight
And grey for the morning and black for the night

He'll paint the long evenings when the light starts to fade
And paint all the bluebells that hide in the shade
And he'll colour the autumn when the wind has turned cold
And paint the leaves falling in copper and gold

He'll paint the hot summer all red like the sun
And he'll ripen to yellow what the winter's undone
And he'll purple the mountain with a heathery hue
And sometimes I wonder will he run out of blue

And sometimes I wonder at the colours he chose
Was green meant for envy and red for the rose
And I'm glad when he'd painted all the blue in the skies
He had some left over for Evelyn's eyes.

MÊL·Y·BONT

'Mêl-y-Bont' was written to print on the labels of honey jars bearing 'The Honey of the "Bont"'.

I wrote it for my old friend, Michael Griffiths, who was an avid beekeeper and a past player with Glynneath, Neath and Aberavon.

Michael was suffering with motor neurone disease, but the support he had from so many of his friends and family is indicative of the love and affection we all had for this great man, who fought his illness with great courage and dignity.

The 'Bont' is a shortened name for the little village of **Pont***neddfechan, 'the bridge of the little river Neath', near to where Michael once lived.*

The Sweetest of Honey from the nectar of flowers
The harvest of bees, from the summer's long hours
Its taste will beguile you, its fragrance will haunt
'A gift' you can treasure
From the bees of the Bont.

Since I wrote 'Mêl-y-Bont', Michael has sadly passed away. This is one verse of a poem I wrote that was read out at Michael's funeral.

A tribute to my friend . . . the bee keeper:

Who'll Tell the Bees

What can you say when you lose an old friend
Who gathered the sun when it shone
For the ones that you leave find it hard to believe
And who'll tell the bees that you've gone . . .

Mêl-y Bont

Honey

454g

SIRHOWY HILL

'Sirhowy Hill' is a song which gets its title from the valley of the same name. It was written while I was reflecting on the threatened closure of the steel works in the south Wales valleys near Tredegar and Ebbw Vale. The fact that flowers were growing again on the hills was no compensation to the steelworker faced with unemployment, but was proof in itself that the wheel had turned full circle for the men of a valley long forged in a skill.

A steel town was waking as dawn was breaking
And talk was uneasy 'bout things at the Mill
And talk is uneasy in the streets of the valley
For flowers are growing on a Sirhowy Hill.

CHORUS
For the wheel is full turning
And flowers are learning
To grow once again
On a Sirhowy Hill.

I wandered my way on that shabby old morning
In a broken old valley where the pitwheel is still
Where tired old terraces built in a hurry
Are painted so gaily on a Sirhowy Hill.

The smoke and the sulphur I knew as a lad
On thinking it over, it wasn't that bad
So let those old furnaces do what they will
Now flowers are growing on Sirhowy Hill.

Those hills that were crippled of hawthorn and heather
Of fern and of flower strangely are still
For the wheel is full turning and flowers are learning
To grow once again on Sirhowy Hill.

They'll sit and decide in the seats of decision
On the fate of a valley should the furnaces chill
And offer new work in some marshmallow factory
To men of a valley long forged in a skill.

THE SEAGULLS OF LLANDUDNO

This is a song I wrote for a television 'In Concert' programme which came from Llandudno in north Wales. There had been a move in the town to cull all the seagulls' eggs and burn their nests in an attempt to cut down on the number of seabirds nesting in the town. It was argued by some hoteliers that

The gulls were a nuisance
The gulls were a pest
Smash all their eggs
Destroy every nest.

They claimed that holidaymakers were tempted not to return to Llandudno because of the seagulls. Many letters were received by the local newspaper concerning the problem, arguing both for and against, the 'Seagulls of Llandudno'.

In a town called Llandudno, so the Tourist Board say
There's safe sandy beaches for the children to play
There's a prom and a pier and a cafe or two
And a towering headland with a breathtaking view.

CHORUS
Tooraloo, Tooralay
Come to Llandudno the Tourist Board say.

But the town has a problem, all is not well
Seagulls are nesting in every hotel
The gulls are a nuisance, complain all the guests
Smash all their eggs and destroy all their nests.

When I came last summer, I remember it well
I booked bed and breakfast in a four-star hotel
I asked them to wake me, a call about ten
They told me, 'Don't worry, you'll be awake before then.'

An old lady told me she went there to rest
And she didn't find that the gulls were a pest
I asked, 'Don't they wake you at dawn every day?'
She answered me, 'Pardon, what did you say?'

'It's a job for the council,' said some in the town
'They should dress up as seagulls and shoot the bird down.'
'No! No!' said the Mayor, 'You never can tell,
The chance is we'll shoot at each other as well!'

A man up from Bangor he walked in the street
When a herring gull had him from ten thousand feet
His wife passed him paper to wipe up his brow
He said, 'It's no good, love, he's miles away now.'

And now as I'm leaving the truth I will tell
I'm fond of those seagulls and I'll bid them
    farewell
And to those who complain and there's
    more than a few
Just you remember – they were here
    before you!

THE STORY OF CHRISTMAS

In our town every Christmas we all play a part
Retelling the magical story
Of how to a mother a baby was born
In a stable so bare and so lonely
And that story is told at this time every year
When shepherds on hillsides are filled with such fear
It's a memory of Christmas I still hold so dear
Retelling the story of Christmas

CHORUS
And the band played 'Come, All Ye Faithful'
As we painted our bright shining star
And the story we told was more precious than gold
That the wise men had brought from afar

I remember the face of a mother and child
And the joy to the earth they were bringing
And the mothers of Angels who all knew the words
Of the songs their children were singing
And they sang of a child who in swaddling was found
And they watched the young shepherds sit fearful around
As the dressing-gown kings lay their gifts on the ground
As we retold the story of Christmas

And the band played 'Come, All Ye Faithful'
As we painted our bright shining star
And the story we told was more precious than gold
That the wise men had brought from afar

And now every Christmas we still play the part
Retelling the magical story
Of how to a mother a baby was born
In a stable so bare and so lonely
And I watch from my window that same shining star
That the wise men had seen and had followed so far
And we sang 'Three Kings from the Orient Are' . . .
As we retold the story of Christmas

And the band played 'Come, All Ye Faithful'
As we painted our bright shining star
And the story we told was more precious than gold
That the wise men had brought from afar

I GUESS IT'S BEEN ONE OF THEM DAYS
(THE SADDEST *EVER* COUNTRY SONG)

I was born out in Utah in a tumbledown shack
Some chickens out the front and some pigs out the back
My folks ploughed the land, raised cattle and all
Till Ma caught the fever and died in the fall

CHORUS
I guess it's been one of them days
I guess it's been one of them days
There's no use in crying and there's no use in sighing
I guess it's been one of them days

So we burnt my Ma's clothes should the fever it spread
Her old wedding dress and her old feather bed
The boots that she wore and her apron and gown
And a spark from the fire, it burnt the barn down

The long winter passed and old Pa, he got tired
'Cos we'd lost all we had in that terrible fire
Then the crops they all failed in a summer of drought
'Cos we used all the water to put the blaze out

Then Pa turned to gambling and he lost everything
So he told me to pawn things like Ma's wedding ring
Then Pa, he turned outlaw so that I could get fed
But I'd pawned his gun and he got shot in the head

They locked up my Pa but he bust out again
Robbed a bank up in Denver and held up a train
Then he headed for home with the money he'd stashed
And a mile from our homestead that old engine, she crashed
  (whoo whoo)

She ploughed down the mountain and the driver got killed
Went right through the bar, which I'd just had rebuilt
Ploughed through a field and into a bog
And Pa, he got drowned along with his dog

Well they buried my Pa and I grieved at our loss
And when the preacher struck up with 'The Old Rugged Cross'
And I cried when the band played a sad country song
And when I saw on his tombstone . . .
They'd spelt his name wrong

JOHNNY MILDEW AND THE SCUM

I have always enjoyed writing and performing humorous, topical songs; so when the 'New Wave' swept through Britain, 'Johnny Mildew and the Scum' were formed. (The first Welsh Punk Band.)

It was a complete departure from anything I had previously written, and we all had great fun recording the song for my 'In Concert' television series. However, some people took it seriously and after the programme was transmitted I received letters begging me 'not to change'. I found it unbelievable that it could be taken seriously, but then even my aunt remarked after watching the programme: 'I didn't like that group you had on with you last week.'

Now I was born in Merthyr.
I didn't want to stay
There was nowhere I could go
There was nowhere I could play
So we moved away to Cardiff
To where they'd understand
That we were a 'New Wave Punk Rock Band'.

We got ourselves an agent
A Dowlais man named Dai
He got us an audition
With a chap from EMI
He said, 'We'll give you kids a break
The public's kinda dumb
And we'll call you Johnny Mildew
And we'll call the band "The Scum".'

We played the pubs in Cardiff
To earn ourselves some bread
I wore my trousers inside out
And dyed my hair all red
I wrote myself some songs
Like 'I'm into sniffing glue'
And 'I love you so much baby –
I could spit all over you!'

I wore my punk rock clothes
Chains and safety pins
And made a coat from stuff
That they use to line the bins
I stood in a shop doorway
With a pin right through my lip
And a refuse lorry saw me
And I ended on a tip.

We brought a record out last week
I couldn't understand
The BBC won't play it
Producers had it banned
The chorus is offensive
Some words they'll have to 'bleep'
It goes '***********'*

Our record contract's folded
They've had enough, I guess
But we've had offers from the States
To sign for CBS
We'll make a big impression
When we get over there
We'll scream abuse
And spill our juice
And tell them – 'We don't care.'

---

* Publisher's note: This line has been censored.

THE BALLAD OF MORGAN THE MOON

The Americans claim they were the first to land on the moon. This song argues differently and tells the story of that pioneering pipe fitter, Morgan Jones, who was known throughout the valley as 'Morgan the Moon'.

Old Mog the mechanic, I remember him well.
He once built a rocket, or so they will tell,
From an old winding-engine he found on the dole,
Built in the Rhondda and powered by coal.

And when it was finished he painted it red,
And he called it *Bethania*, or so it is said.
And he took it up a mountain on a night late in June
'To get that bit closer,' said Morgan the Moon.

Sleepy Treorchy was bathed in white light
When the shuddering hulk took off in the night.
A deafening scream and then a great roar,
And up past the houses old Morgan did go.

His heat-shield was glowing like anthracite coal
And we prayed down in Cardiff, in mission control.
The barrow-wheels dropped as was previously planned
And old Morgan prepared for *Bethania* to land.

He landed like linen on a crusty old crater:
Dai said he'd get there lunar or later!
So off Morgan went in the moon's swirling dust,
To collect some rock samples from a crater's hard crust.

A strange piece of rock soon old Morgan found,
Just lying there shining on the dust-covered ground.
He picked it up closely and he let out a call
'Cos written right through it in Welsh was 'Porthcawl'!

THE BOY WHO CLIMBED A MOUNTAIN

Here's to Geraint Thomas, who rode and took his chance
The boy who climbed a mountain and won the Tour de France.

There's a pillar box in Cardiff, where the mayor has arranged
To buy some tins of yellow paint, and have the colour changed
And down in Cardiff City Hall, I heard the council say
We'll change the name of the Severn Bridge to the Geraint
    Thomas Way.

Now Whitchurch High are rightly proud, and love to tell the tale
How he carved his name in the wood of a desk, like Warburton
    and Bale
And where his yellow jersey hangs, beside the wooden beams
'The boy who climbed a mountain', and dared to chase his
    dreams.

But there were some who doubted. 'He doesn't stand a chance!'
There's never been a Welshman who's won the Tour de France
But he's more than just a *domestique*, I've known it all along
The boy deserves a knighthood and his bike deserves a gong.

That day we'll long remember, and I'll oft recall that night
When the Senedd and the castle walls were bathed in yellow light
And I saw the round moon smiling from on its jealous height
And turn its face to yellow in the dark of Cardiff's night.

And I hope he'll make a fortune, and saves up for a yacht
And buys a second home in France, and a *pied-à-terre* in Splott
But I know that fame won't change him, and to me that's such
    a joy
'Cos though he lives in Monaco, he's still a Cardiff boy.

In the Grogg shop up in Ponty, they're working night and day
The kilns are full of Geraints, but there's such a long delay
There're queues of people waiting and the owner told me why
Geraint's gone and grown his hair and it takes so long to dry.

So I'll buy a Grogg of Geraint, although they don't come cheap
And I'll sell my one of Elvis, and one of Lynn the Leap
'Cos when G rode through Paris, and waved to all the crowd
He more than climbed a mountain, he made a nation proud.

I hope it's fine on Thursday, though I think it's still in doubt
So Derek has suggested that we keep our brollies out
So I'll stand outside the City Hall, with its gilded marble dome
And sing like England football fans that 'Geraint's coming home'.

THE RICHEST DUST

As a lifelong supporter of Glamorgan County Cricket Club, I was thrilled to see a Test match between England and Australia being played at Cardiff's Sophia Gardens.

There were some doubters who thought it would be over in three days on a turning pitch.

Not that it hasn't happened before . . .

Way back in 1882 down Lambeth's leafy ways
When Hornbury's feted English side were beaten in two days,
A venting spleen in *The Sporting Times* wrote scornful of the failure
'The cremated bodies' ashes will be taken to Australia.'
Then Captain Ivo Bligh proud stood and took a lordly stand
And vowed the ashes would return to his green and pleasant land.
But that summer found him wanting and still mournful of his loss,
Some ashes with respect bequeathed beneath the Southern Cross.
The outer casing of a ball? A broken stump or bail?
The splintered hopes of England's dreams? Or an aging mother's veil?
The questions without answer and may we never learn
The secret of the Ashes in that terracotta urn.
And now a 100 years have passed and I'm weary of the dross
That's written in some papers about English cricket's loss!
'The first Test on a turning pitch', it will be over in two days,
Just like it was in '82, down Lambeth's leafy ways.
So if England win at Cardiff we'll cremate the stumps and bails
And the richest dust in England will forever be in Wales!

TIME

Time is a present that cannot be bought
Time can be endless, time can be short
Time can be cruel, time can be kind
Time is a gift the past's left behind
Time's like a river that flows from the deep
And runs on for ever with us in its keep

YNG NGOFAL DY FREICHIAU DI
(IN THE SHELTER OF YOUR ARMS)

This poem/song is the first I can remember writing (I have since improved it). It tells of a mother's love and how, when the sun was setting and the night was darkening in the Black Mountains, she'd come and sit in the stillness of night and keep one safe till morning light.

Pan fo'r haul yn machlud ar y gorwel
Ar nôs yn twyllu draw dros y Mynydd Du
Fe ddoi di draw i aros yn y llonydd
A dal fi'n saff yng ngofal dy freichiau di

PART TWO
THE
STORIES

BERWYN'S SKULL

One of the great characters I have written about over the years is my old friend Berwyn, who hails from the little village of Rosehill near Cardigan in west Wales.

He's a hill farmer but he could be found every Sunday morning at the car boot sale in one of the local farmer's fields, Cae'r Bont. He'd sell brass candlesticks, wax flowers, old paintings, porcelain and all manner of bric-à-brac.

One Sunday an American couple from Chicago of Welsh ancestry were visiting the 'old country' and they came across Berwyn at the car boot sale.

The American, searching around in Berwyn's bric-à-brac, noticed among the Swansea porcelain a . . . human skull . . . and he enquired, 'Please, sir, may I ask whose skull is that?'

'That,' said Berwyn, 'is the skull of Owain Glyndŵr, the last native Prince of Wales.'

'Oh my God,' exclaimed the American. 'You mean Owen Glendower?'

'The very one,' said Berwyn.

'My God, did you hear that, honey? The skull of Owen Glendower. I'd love to purchase that and take it back to the USA and show it to the Cymmrodorion Society in Chicago. How much do you want for such an historical artefact?'

'One thousand pounds,' said Berwyn. 'Plus VAT.'

'Then, sir, you have a deal.' . . . Oh my God! *Cymru am byth* . . . !

Berwyn wrapped the skull up carefully and added, 'If I may say, a wise investment, a shrewd purchase that can only increase in value with time.'

A few years later the American was over in Wales for a family funeral. Once again he visited the car boot sale at Cae'r Bont Farm, and there was Berwyn as usual selling brass candlesticks, wax flowers, old paintings and porcelain, and the American noticed among the bric-à-brac a small human skull.

He enquired of Berwyn, 'Please tell me, sir, whose skull is *that*?'

Berwyn replied proudly but in hushed tones, 'That, my friend, is the skull of the last Prince of Wales, Owain Glyndŵr . . .'

'But that can't be,' exclaimed the American. '*I* bought the skull of Owen Glendower some years ago and that one is *much* smaller.'

'Yes,' said Berwyn. 'That was when he was a boy . . .'

BERWYN AND THE AEROPLANE RIDE

One of my favourite stories about Berwyn is when he went for a first ride in an aeroplane.

He had always dreamt of a ride in a small aircraft, so on his eighteenth birthday his father took him to Cardiff Airport, where you could book flights on small private aircraft.

Berwyn was so excited when they taxied down the small runway in a four-seater, twin-propeller Cessna Sky Hawk with a range of 640 miles.

They took off and flew over Cardiff Airport, tears of joy streaming down young Berwyn's face.

Thirty minutes later, they landed back at the airport and Berwyn said excitedly, 'Oh, I enjoyed that so much, Dad, but it went so quickly. Can I go up again, Dad . . . ?'

His father said, 'I'm sorry, Berwyn, I can't afford another hundred pounds. We're only struggling hill farmers.'

The owner and pilot of the Cessna, retired Wing Commander Henry (Biggles) Smythe, approached Berwyn and his father and said,

'I hope you don't mind but I overheard your conversation with Berwyn and I have a proposition to make to you. I'll take you *both* up in my Cessna Sky Hawk and if you remain absolutely silent during the flight . . . I won't charge you.'

Berwyn's father, a shrewd man of Cardigan (known to be careful with their money) turned to Berwyn and said, 'Did you hear that? If we remain absolutely silent during the flight we won't have to pay. So not a word, Berwyn . . . *Dim Gair* . . . Not a word.'

The little aircraft took off flying into the sun and climbed to 13,000 feet. It began a series of belly rolls and death dives before flying *under* the Severn Bridge, narrowly missing some 33 kV pylons and Aberthaw Power Station and Cement Works before landing safely back at the airstrip.

Captain Henry Smythe got out, removed his flying goggles and said to Berwyn's father, 'May I say, Mr Morgan, I've been pulling this stunt, this wheeze, for many years and *no one* has remained absolutely silent during the flight before. Tell me, Mr Morgan, out of interest, was there any moment when you nearly said something?'

'Oh! Yes,' said Mr Morgan . . . 'When Berwyn fell out.'

GRAVESTONE FOR SALE

That story about Berwyn's first ride in an aeroplane seems to perpetuate the myth that the Cardis (people from Cardigan) are careful with their money.

I always thought it was totally wrong until I saw an advert in the *Cambrian News* . . .

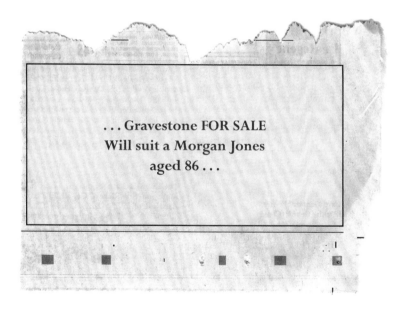

. . . Gravestone FOR SALE
Will suit a Morgan Jones
aged 86 . . .

BERWYN'S PHOTO

I remember the time when Berwyn's brother Idris died and Berwyn wanted to put a nice photo of him on the family piano, but he only had a small faded black-and-white one taken at the Royal Welsh Show, with his arm around some prizewinning livestock.

Anyway, undaunted he took the photograph to a photographic shop in Cardiff specialising in creative and innovative digital photography.

He asked the manager could he introduce some colour into the image and increase it in size.

The manager said, 'That will be no problem, sir. We do that sort of thing all the time. Is there anything else you want enhanced or altered?'

'Well,' said Berwyn, 'as you can see, he's got his arm around an old bullock in the photo . . . Is there any way you can get rid of that old bullock? I don't want him on the piano with his arm around an old bullock.'

'Well, once again,' said the manager, 'we can erase any part of the image with our Adobe Photoshop software and replace it with something more appropriate. Anything else? I am rather busy.'

'Yes,' said Berwyn. 'His wellington boots. They're full of mud from the show and I don't want him on the piano with muddy boots.'

'Well, what I suggest,' said the manager, 'we could superimpose a small brick wall in front of where your brother is standing and that would then hide his muddy boots and no one would be any the wiser.'

'A little brick wall, that would be brilliant.'

'Is that it?'

'One more thing. His hair, can you cut his hair, or do something with it? It's like a haystack.'

'Well as I'm sure you'll appreciate, sir, we can't actually cut your brother's hair, but with careful airbrushing and our innovative technology we could thin it out somewhat. Tell me, in the interest of authenticity, for we take pride in our attention to detail, on which side did your brother part his hair?'

'Oh!' said Berwyn. 'Let me think now. Um . . . I can't remember . . . Which side . . . ?'

'I'm afraid I'll have to hurry you, sir, I have other clients to meet and time is precious.'

'Oh, I'll tell you what,' said Berwyn, 'to save time . . . *put a cap on him*.'

HOP ON/HOP OFF

I remember when Berwyn had a job with Cardiff City Council as a tour guide on one of those 'hop on/hop off' buses that went around the city, pointing out to visitors historical and important places.

He had a uniform, a peaked cap and a roving microphone connected to a loudspeaker in the bus.

He enjoyed explaining to all the tourists from all over the world the sights and sounds of the City of Cardiff, the Capital City – 'We are now approaching Cardiff City Hall, built in 1906 out of Portland stone in the Edwardian Baroque style and a Grade I listed building.

'On the right-hand side you will be passing Cardiff Castle. Following the death of the 4th Marquess of Bute the family donated the castle and most of its grounds to the City of Cardiff.

'And now we leave the castle walls behind and travel down Westgate Street where on the right-hand side you will see one of, if not *the* most famous, rugby grounds in the world: Cardiff Arms Park.

'It was here in 1922 that Wales beat England 28–6.

'It was here in 1959 that Wales won again 5–0.

'And then again some years later in 1977 Wales beat England 14–9.'

This English chap at the back of the bus interrupted Berwyn and somewhat indignantly said, 'Surely there must have been a time when England won?'

Berwyn blinked and said to him, 'Not on *my* bus . . . !'

CHILDHOOD MEMORIES

I'll ne'er forget those childhood days
E'en when the mem'ry fails
I'll always fond remember
Those times I played for Wales.

In the mining valleys in which I was brought up everybody has played for Wales; few, however, have actually pulled on the scarlet jersey and run on to Cardiff Arms Park, but we've all played at some time or other.

We had our own 'national stadiums' in streets and in back lanes and on bits of waste ground behind welfare halls, where rubbish bins became goalposts and tin sheets became corner flags.

They were multi-purpose grounds, for in the summer they became 'The Oval' and 'Lords' and other famous Test-cricket grounds. The 'goalposts' became wickets, the tin sheets became the sightscreens and Clive Davies's father's garage became the Pavilion end.

One of my friends, Owen Phillips, was the finest 'street' opening bat I have ever seen. He used to draw the wickets with white chalk on the back door of his house. When you claimed you'd 'bowled' him he'd deny it, saying, 'There's no chalk on the ball!'

I'd never argue (he was bigger than me) with the result that before the 'out in the gardens' rule was introduced he was 'in' once for fourteen weeks. I forget how much he scored, but I know we lost . . .

But it was rugby we played most . . .

I'll always remember the first time I played for Wales – it was in Llewellyn Street, I was nine at the time and it was against England (it was always against England). I remember we had twenty-eight on our side and . . . three on their side. It wasn't fair but it was my ball!

I remember we won 406–12 in one of those games where you played four hours each way and only stopped when a ball went under a lorry. In that game I scored twenty-three tries before I was carried off injured: I was late tackled into touch three yards short of my anorak.

We went on to beat Ireland and Scotland – before three o'clock. We would have beaten France as well but Mel Thomas kicked the ball into Mrs Harries's garden and she wouldn't let us have it back. She was a funny woman (from Cardiff). We had her back though – we woke her tortoise up and gave it to this drunk and told him it was a pie.

So then I'd run home and play in the back lane behind my house. I used to make rugby posts out of old kidney-bean sticks; for a ball I used to use an old fairy liquid bottle. I was the best kicker of a fairy liquid bottle in all Glamorgan. I could screw kick to touch

and make the top come off. On thinking back, in all those times never once did we lose. We nearly did once: we were losing to England 36–3 with two minutes to go when – lucky – my mother called me for dinner.

ASHES

Once upon a time in a little village in Surrey there lived a little boy named Jack. He lived with his stepmother, a haughty ugly woman. Now she had two ugly sons who used to bully little Jack and make him get out of bed on cold mornings to clean the grate and light the fire. As he sat there on the hearth amongst the cinders they laughed at him and called him Ashes.

One day the two ugly brothers became very excited. They had received a letter from the Rugby Football Union, telling them they had both been selected for the final English trial. The stepmother was delighted, she had always hoped that one day one of her sons would play for England.

The day of the trial arrived and the tears ran down Jack's little face as he watched them get into their car and drive to Twickenham.

'I wish I could have a trial,' he said.

Then all of a sudden a strange light appeared in the sky and the room was filled with twinkling stars and moonbeams and a little voice said, 'Don't be afraid, Ashes, I am your fairy Godselector and I have come to help you and see that you play in the final English trial, too.'

'But I haven't got any boots,' said Ashes, 'and how will I get to the ground?'

The fairy took Ashes into the garden and asked him to get a pumpkin. He brought one to her and she tapped it with her wand. Suddenly it changed into an Austin Allegro with a pair of brand new rugby boots on the back seat.

'Now,' said the fairy, 'you can play in the trial too.'

But before he left, the fairy warned Ashes that he must return before the clock struck midnight – when all the magic would disappear.

Meanwhile at the final English trial at Twickenham the English selectors were watching without interest the dull, unimaginative play of the probable three-quarters.

Then Ashes ran on to the field and, gathering the loose rolling ball, started to run. The crowd were buzzing with excitement, never before had they seen such a player; he was the sole topic of conversation on the terraces.

After the game was over Ashes was so busy signing autographs in the clubhouse that he forgot all about his promise to the fairy. All at once he heard a clock striking midnight. He realised what was going to happen at any second. Without any explanation to the English selectors he ran out of the ground across to his car.

The clock continued to strike. He ran as fast as he could. In his haste one of his boots came off. The English selectors ran after him, but just as Ashes reached the gates of the ground the clock struck twelve and the only person left outside the ground was a traffic warden sticking a parking ticket on a pumpkin.

The chairman of the English selectors was heartbroken but he made up his mind to search all over England until he found the player whose foot fitted the boot. After much searching he finally came to the house where Ashes lived. Whilst the two ugly brothers laughed, Ashes tried on the boot. It was a perfect fit. The chairman of selectors was overjoyed. At last they had found the answer to all their problems.

But then a strange light appeared in the sky. The room was filled with twinkling stars and moonbeams as Ashes' fairy Godselector appeared again.

'I fear, sirs,' she said to them,
'Young Ashes cannot play.
His stepbrothers tried to tell you
But you brushed them both away
He cannot play for England.'
She waved her wand in anger,
'His father was born in Cardiff
And his mother comes from Bangor.'

Then Ashes said, 'I'll play for Wales.'
'Twas said with fierce pride
But what with Gareth Edwards
He didn't get in the side.

DID HE SUFFER?

A tremendous source of humour is to be found in the comments of the 'characters' that frequent the terraces of football matches.

I remember when J.P.R. Williams, the Welsh full-back, gathered an awkward rolling ball against Scotland in 1976 and the Scottish wing raced up to tackle him. A Scottish voice shouted from the crowd, 'Worry him! Worry him!' A well-oiled Welsh voice replied from the bowels of the North Enclosure, 'Tell him his mother's ill.'

I'll always remember the first time I went to Dublin to see Wales play Ireland. On the Friday morning we were taken by some friends to visit the Guinness factory. Unfortunately one of the lads who was a bit 'under the weather' slipped on an iron-grilled gangway and fell into a thousand-gallon vat of foaming Guinness and drowned.

On the Saturday morning a BBC Wales news reporter interviewed one of my friends, Billy Williams, who had witnessed the accident. 'Mr Williams, all Wales has been grief-stricken by the sad news of this most unfortunate accident. Can you shed perhaps some small crumb of comfort and tell us, did he suffer? Was it, in fact, a painful death?'

'Oh, no!' Billy said. 'He got out three times for a pee!'

THE ONE O'CLOCK GUN

When we were up at Edinburgh for the Scotland–Wales rugby international a few years ago we visited Edinburgh Castle on the Saturday morning before the game. Apparently it's the tradition at Edinburgh Castle to fire what they call the 'one o'clock gun', a great cannon which stands on the ramparts of the castle.

Way down below in Princes Street, thousands of red-and-white scarved Welsh rugby supporters thronged their way through the crowds. One of them, however, had made his way up to the castle. I think he was a Neath supporter for he carried a bedraggled banner on which he had written, 'Even God is Afraid of Brian Thomas'. As he staggered along, the 'one o'clock gun' was fired. He stopped, blinked and went over to the Scot who had fired the cannon and said, 'Take it easy with that cannon pal, there's some of our boys down there!'

THE REV. GORONWY ROBERTS

A few years ago I was playing rugby for Glynneath Athletic (they were short), when twenty minutes into the first half we were awarded a penalty. Our full-back, a North Walian by the name of Dyfnallt Morgan, took the kick and his well-struck attempt hit the upright.

He shook his head and said, 'Bloody hell!'

The referee, the Rev. Goronwy Roberts (Llwynhendy), admonished him saying, 'There is no need to swear.' Dyfnallt apologised and then a few minutes later we were awarded another penalty. Dyfnallt took great care but unfortunately his second attempt veered away at the last second and struck the other upright.

'Bloody hell!' he exclaimed.

The Rev. Goronwy Roberts went across to him and said, 'I've told you once – there is no need to swear. If you feel the sap of anger rising, just pause for a second and say "Help me, Lord" and that moment of anger surely will pass.'

By this time we were losing 16–14 with only minutes to go, when we were awarded yet another kick at goal. This time from in front of the posts. The crowd hushed as Dyfnallt with great deliberation made his mark, took three measured steps back, allowed for the cross wind and . . . sliced it!

The ball went skidding away towards the corner flag. Dyfnallt shook his head and was about to say … when he remembered and said, 'Help me, Lord!'

The skies darkened, there was the sound of a mighty rushing wind and a strange light appeared in the sky. The ball shuddered in flight, changed direction and went between the posts and the Rev. Goronwy Roberts said, 'Bloody hell!'

AUSTRALIA '78

When I was in Australia during the Welsh rugby tour of 1978 I met a remarkable Welshwoman who came to every concert I appeared in and to every game that Wales played in Australia. On the eve of the last test in Sydney she turned up at the theatre with two warm Welsh faggots for me. When I thanked her, she explained that she also had thirty more for the Welsh team and asked where the team were staying. I told her and she went round there at half past eight on the Saturday morning before the game with thirty warm Welsh faggots. Clive Rowlands, the team manager, accepted the gift and assured her that the 'boys' would have them for breakfast.

As events turned out we lost the last test and in the after-match function the first person I met was this woman, her eyes all swollen red, tears streaming down her face.

'Oh, Max!' she said. 'Did you see the game?'

I answered that I had and told her not to be upset.

'Oh, Max!' she said. 'Do you think it was the faggots?'

WHERE ARE YOU FROM?

During a rugby international at Cardiff, with singing ringing from the terraces, an American tourist turned to some Welsh supporters and asked in a real Southern drawl, 'Where is this choir from?'

One of the lads laughed, 'They're not a choir. They're just ordinary supporters like us.'

'Tell me then,' asked the Yank, 'where are you from?'

He said, 'I'm from Llangyfelach.'

'Yeah,' the Yank went on, 'but what state, what zip code?'

The Welsh supporter turned to me and asked (in Welsh), 'What is this one talking about – I've told him once, I'm from Llangyfelach!'

'Oh,' I explained, 'what you perhaps don't realise is that this chap's from America and he's probably never heard of Llangyfelach.'

'Damn! I didn't think of that,' he said, so he went back to the Yank and told him, 'I'm from Llangyfelach . . . three miles from Morriston.'

'IN THESE STONES . . .'

I'm very proud that the *first-ever* public performance at the Millennium Centre in Cardiff was 'MAX BOYCE in Concert', and my special guest was a relatively unknown opera singer, Katherine Jenkins, who went on to greatness.

I remember standing outside the theatre and reading Gwyneth Lewis's inspiring words on the front of the building,

CREU GWIR FEL GWYDR O FFWRNAIS AWEN
IN THESE STONES HORIZONS SING

when a little boy no more than five years old came up to me and said, 'Mister, I know what those big words on that building says.'

'That's clever of you,' I replied. 'What do they say?'

He said, 'ASDA . . .!'

WHAT'S THAT HE'S CARRYING?

I had performed at the very first Royal Command Performance in Wales at the New Theatre in Cardiff in front of Prince Charles and Lady Diana, and subsequently I was asked to perform at the Royal Command Performance at the London Palladium in 1978 in front of the Queen Mother.

I was naturally nervous. I ran on to the stage of the most famous variety theatre in the world carrying an enormous leek and wearing a Welsh rugby scarf and bobble hat . . .

I can see them now. A stiff couple sat in the front row who hadn't smiled all night looked at me with bewilderment.

The wife turned to her husband and asked,

'I say, darling, *what's that* he's carrying?'

He said, 'I don't know . . . I think it's a spring onion!'

'What do you think he's going to do with it?'

'I don't know . . .'

And then he whispered something in her ear, and she said,

'Oh, I hope so . . .'

ELI JENKINS

Many years ago now, my local chapel, 'The Addoldy', asked me to help raise some money to repair the roof of the chapel and help maintain the graveyard.

I agreed and suggested I organise some sort of show.

After some thought I came up with the idea of putting on Dylan Thomas's *Under Milk Wood*.

I would wear a wig and a moustache and play every character in Dylan's play for voices – first voice Organ Morgan, Polly Garter, Willy Nilly, Captain Cat and of course the Rev. Eli Jenkins – all in different voices and accents of his ugly, lovely town.

To make it more theatrical I ran some cables from the pulpit to lights I'd installed in various parts of the chapel – behind the clock, under the organ and in the upstairs pews. Then I connected everything to a dimmer switch, which I could use to create theatrical effects when appropriate.

When I got to Eli Jenkins's Prayer and the line, '. . . and in the evening when the sun goes down I ask a blessing on this town . . .', I'd press the dimmer switch hidden in the recesses of the pulpit and the red light behind the clock upstairs would fade to an orange glow.

I was on my feet for two and a half hours *without* a note or *any* prompt playing *every* part with total commitment and with no little passion.

After the performance, we were in the vestry of the little chapel and this woman came up to my mother and said, 'Oh! He was good. He was outstanding . . . Tell me, Mrs Boyce, was he like that when he was a boy?'

'Oh! Yes,' my mother said, 'anything electric.'

LEEKES CROSS HANDS

In the late seventies, I was asked to officially open the Leekes furniture store in Cross Hands near Llanelli.

Mr Gerald Leeke OBE, now a dear friend, explained how I'd be picked up by helicopter at Glynneath Rugby Club's ground, Abernant Park, and taken to Cross Hands.

He also explained that there would be onboard two actors dressed as SuperTed and Spotty Man to entertain the children during the official opening.

No one in the village knew this was happening, and just before the helicopter landed, a lovely old Irishman – and a lifelong member of the rugby club – was passing on his bike and noticed the helicopter hovering overhead.

'That's the way to travel, Max,' he said.

'Yes, Phil,' I said. 'I'll call him down now.'

The helicopter landed in a swirl of dust and blades, and Spotty Man and SuperTed got out, came across to greet me and helped me to board the aircraft.

Phil couldn't believe his eyes and exclaimed in a thick Irish accent, 'Jesus . . . Mother of God . . .'

He peddled as fast as he could up to the rugby club, burst into the bar . . . and shouted, 'C'mon quick, boys . . . Come quick, aliens have got Max . . . !'

WHAT GOES AROUND COMES AROUND

During my first concert tour of South Africa in 1995 I was invited by a South African farmer, Otto Raynbeck, to visit his home in KwaZulu-Natal.

He proudly showed me his 'trophy' room and the wild animals that his family had hunted and killed in the 'bush'. He said, 'Max, see that there. That's a white-tailed gnu . . . My grandfather killed that with a rifle on the open plains of the Free State.

'And that one there is the greater kudu, with its unique markings and majestic spiral horns. My grandfather killed that in the Bushveld with a crossbow.

'And that there, Max, as I'm sure you know is a leopard, the smallest of the big five but the most elusive and difficult to hunt. But my grandfather killed it with a single shot in the grassland savanna.

'And the last one there, Max, is the rhino, weighing around *four tonnes*. We had to use eight-inch coach screws to secure it to the wall . . .

'But that rhino, Max . . . killed my grandfather . . . !'

'Oh!' I said. 'I'm sorry to hear that. Did it charge him?'

'No! The screws came loose and it fell on him . . . !'

L'ESCARGOT

I have great and lasting memories of the Five Nations rugby tournament and many of my songs reflect that.

One I love to retell is when my neighbour went to France to see Wales play at the Parc des Princes in the 1970s with several new caps and Wales unexpectedly won.

Ron met some boys from Wales and they started on the red wine . . . a rough, cheap country wine. Not used to red wine, some hours later Ron was carried to his bed . . . singing 'I'm a Little Teapot'.

Needless to say Ron missed his plane home in the morning. He blamed the hotel and told his wife they hadn't given him an early morning call.

As a result he wasn't allowed to go again, but time is a great healer and some twenty years later he was forgiven and he told his wife, 'I won't do that again. I was so wrong. I shouldn't have drunk so much. But I'll make it up to you. I'll bring you some Moët & Chandon champagne and some French perfume. I won't let you down again.'

'I don't want champagne or perfume,' she said. 'Just come back the same time as everybody else and bring me back some fresh Burgundy snails that you can only get in the markets in Paris. And try and get them in their shells.'

'Right!' said Ron, and fair play, as soon as we landed he went straight to this fish market in Paris to buy some snails.

He bought twenty-four in their shells for ten euros and put them in a hessian bag. They never left his side . . . He even took them to the game, which Wales won.

Not having learnt his lesson, Ron was back on the red wine and he didn't get home till the following Tuesday.

He got to his home at three o'clock in the morning and tried to creep in without waking his wife.

He eased the front door key into the lock, quietly pushed open the door . . . and stood on the cat . . . who bounded off screeching.

Ron dropped his hessian bag of snails. It split open and the snails spilled out, rolling all over the stone floor outside his house.

The landing light came on and there was Ron's wife at the top of the stairs . . . the War department.

'Well, Ron,' she said, 'what's your excuse this time?'

Ron turned to the snails and said, 'C'mon boys, not far now . . . !'

BASTILLE LOUIS XV

When we were in France one time one of my pals, Idris, was condemned to death by the guillotine (another case of mistaken identity). There we were on the Monday morning after the match in this French prison, 'Bastille Louis XV'. This French guard with a black hood over his head approached Idris and said (in French), 'It is the tradition of this prison to grant the condemned prisoner one last request before he dies – what is your request?'

Idris thought for a moment and then he said, 'I am a proud Welshman and I'd like to sing a song before I die.'

The French guard nodded. 'You are a brave man, *monsieur*. You may sing your song.'

And there in that Bastille surrounded by cold, grey, unfriendly walls, Idris began to sing:

'One hundred thousand million green bottles …'

A TRUE STORY

One fateful day the phone rings in my home in Glynneath.

Brr brr brr . . .

'Hello, it's Edward Windsor here. Can I possibly speak to Mr Max Boyce, please?'

My wife, thinking it was someone from the Windsor Motors garage where my car was being serviced, said, 'Oh, I'm sorry. He's not here at the moment. He's playing golf with Russ and Dai Knoyle but he shouldn't be long. He's going to the match . . . Glynneath are playing Bryncoch in the West Wales Cup . . . and he won't miss that.'

'Thank you. I'll call again later.'

Brr brr brr. The phone rings again.

'Hello. Mr Edward Windsor here. Is it possible to speak with Mr Max Boyce?'

'Oh, I'm awfully sorry. He's not back yet but he shouldn't be long . . . Glynneath are playing Bryncoch in the West Wales Cup.'

'Very well. I'll try a little later.'

This happened twice again and my poor wife was getting embarrassed . . . and didn't want to answer the phone . . .

A few minutes later I burst through the door. 'Where's my coat ? . . . I'm late . . . What's the time?'

My wife said, 'You're not going anywhere till you've spoken to this poor man. He must have rung five times. Where have you been?'

Brr brr brr. The phone rings again.

'You've got to answer that. I'm not speaking to him!'

'Hello. This is Edward Windsor here. Could I possibly speak to Mr Max Boyce?'

'Max here,' I said. 'Can I call you in the morning? I'm very late. I'm going to the match. Glynneath are playing Bryncoch in the West Wales Cup and the boys are waiting for me . . . Can I call you in the morning?'

'I'm afraid not, Mr Boyce. I'm flying to Canada with my mother, the Queen . . .'

It suddenly dawned on me. Edward Windsor . . . Prince Edward . . . !!!

He was acting on behalf of Andrew Lloyd Webber's theatre company, the Really Useful Theatre Co., who wanted me to speak at the launch of his Sydmonton Festival later that year.

I agreed to speak and turned to my wife and said, 'Do you know who you've been speaking to *all* afternoon? . . . Edward Windsor . . . Prince Edward, the Queen's youngest son.'

'Oh! Don't say that,' she said. 'Look at the place. It's like a tip . . . !!'
A few weeks later the phone rings in my house.
'Hello . . . Edward Windsor here. I hope you don't mind me asking but . . . how did Glynneath get off against Bryncoch . . . ?'

IN THE BLEAK MIDWINTER

A few days after I had played the Royal Albert Hall in London I appeared in a rugby club in the village of Brynmawr near Merthyr Tydfil. The organisers were unduly concerned that facilities weren't up to those of the Albert Hall, with the result the Ladies' Committee decided to do something about it. One of them, a lovely friendly lady, had some wallpaper left over from decorating her child's bedroom and had decided to paper my dressing room with it. So there I was, surrounded by teddy bears, golliwogs and trains, and in the corner, a big heavy ironclad cooker.

It was in the middle of winter and extremely cold, so they had dragged this cooker from somewhere and turned all the hot plates on full to heat my dressing room. The chairman came in to enquire if everything was satisfactory. I assured him that it was and thanked him for all his club's efforts.

'That's all right, Max,' he said, 'if you're still cold – put the grill on.'

THE NIGHT OF THE LONG SHOVEL

I've been very lucky over the years not to have had many concerts cancelled because of adverse weather, but in the winter of 2018 we were forced to cancel a few because of really heavy snow.

I was due to appear in concert at the Lyric Theatre, Carmarthen, where the surrounding area was severely affected and the M4 was partially closed.

We tried to get through but the snow was so deep.

We got as far as Cross Hands, around twelve miles from Carmarthen, when we passed a man at the side of the road up to his neck in snow.

We stopped and went to his assistance.

'Hang on in there,' I said. 'I'll go and get a shovel.'

He said, 'Get a long one, Max. I'm on a horse . . .'

IS THAT THE SUN OR THE MOON?

One evening in Pontardulais I saw an old man pointing up to the sky and I overheard him ask his friend, 'Is that the sun or the moon?'

'I'm not sure,' his friend replied, 'we'd better ask that man over there in the bus shelter.'

They approached the man and one of them asked, 'Excuse me, but can you tell us, is that the sun or the moon?'

'I'm not sure,' replied the man, 'I'm from Port Talbot!'

HOW DO I GET TO CARMARTHEN?

I was out walking one day and a car stopped and a very 'English' voice called out to this old collier who happened to be passing. 'Hey Dai, come here. How do I get to Carmarthen?'

The old man walked slowly towards the car and asked, 'How did you know my name was Dai?'

The frightfully English Englishman replied, 'I guessed.'

The old man smiled and said, 'Then guess your way to Carmarthen.'

EVELYN'S CAKE

They say the best stories are the true stories. This is a *true* story that happened December 2018.

My granddaughter Evelyn Grace was celebrating her third birthday and her mother – my daughter Rhiannon – had arranged to have a special birthday cake made for her by a woman who lived in the village of Cilfrew near Neath.

It was a very special cake with three candles and Evelyn's name written in icing on the top.

I was to pick the cake up and take it to my daughter's house in Swansea.

I drove down to Cilfrew on the morning of Evelyn's birthday to find the address I'd been given, 23 _____ Road near Neath.

The first problem I encountered . . . There were no numbers or names on the doors . . .

Undaunted, I knocked on a likely door halfway up the terraced street.

'Excuse me, is this 23 _____ Road?'

'No, love . . . Oooh, look who it is. Oggie oggie! What are you doing here? Wait till I tell our Davy . . . He loves you. He hasn't been very well. He's under the doctor. I'll phone him now. *And we were singing hymns and arias . . .*'

I ask again, 'Is this number 23?'

'No, love. We're number 12. Try across the road. That house with a skip outside.'

I knock on the door. 'Excuse me, is this 23 _____ Road?'

'Ooooh, Bryn, come here quick. It's you, isn't it. Can I have a selfie? It's him, Bryn. Off the telly. I've got all your records. Wait till I tell our Kyle. I'll text her now. Oh my God, Max Boyce . . .'

'Is this number 23?'

'No, love. Try the white house with a Sky van outside. I think that's number 23.'

By now the whole street are out waving and shouting, 'Oggie, oggie, oggie!', phoning their friends and telling their neighbours.

I finally find number 23 . . . and knock on the door.

This woman comes out, her hair in curlers, carrying a young baby with a dummy, recognises me and starts shouting to her friend upstairs, 'Jesus God! Mary, come quick . . . We've won the Postcode Lottery!'

I said, '*No!* I've only come for the cake.'

The street is all out now, singing, '*We're gonna knock on your door, ring on your bell* . . . Couldn't happen to a nicer family.'

I said, 'I've only come for the cake.'

Evelyn's six now . . .

SEVE'S WEDGE

One of the most unforgettable days of my life was playing in the Epson golf tournament at St Pierre near Chepstow. I was invited to play in the pro/am, which preceded the main event.

I had played in a few local pro/ams but nothing quite as prestigious as this with all the top golfers in Europe competing for 1.6 million pounds in prize money.

Now, I have performed at Wembley in front of 80,000 people, at the opening ceremony of the Rugby World Cup and at Sydney Opera House, but nothing compares to standing on the first tee of a major pro/am.

It is a terrifying place to be and not for the faint-hearted. It can be the loneliest place is the world and I have seen seasoned performers crumble, weighed down by expectation. Some have even failed to turn up despite initially accepting the invitation, and hidden in their hotel room . . . till it was dark.

It is where you rediscover your religious beliefs and pray to a kindly God.

'Please, let me just get it away. I promise I'll give any prize money to the "Blind Donkeys of Bethlehem" fund . . . Please, God, let me just get it away.'

But God, for some reason only known to himself, disconnects your brain from the rest of your body . . . and gives you somebody else's arms . . . who's never played before!

Your head is filled with the demons of doubt and you begin to talk to yourself . . . and ask yourself ridiculous questions like,

'Am I right-handed?'

'Of course you are . . .'

'How do you know?'

'You've got right-handed clubs.'

'Oh! Yes, thank God . . .'

Now, I arrived at St Pierre that morning after a restless sleep the night before armed with all the accreditation for the pro/am and secretly hoping I'd been drawn to play with someone relatively unknown so there'd be no great gallery following us.

Imagine the horror when I looked at the draw in the pro/am office . . .

Max Boyce drawn to play with Seve Ballesteros.

SEVE BALLESTEROS . . . Oh no . . . SEVE . . .

I was to partner one of the greatest and certainly the most charismatic golfers the world has ever seen.

I remember standing on the first tee. My legs had turned to jelly and I wanted to go home.

The starter's voice crackled in the loudspeakers.

'And now match number thirteen . . . From Pedreña in Spain, winner of five majors, including two green jackets at the Masters in Augusta, Mr Seve Ballesteros. And playing alongside Seve, from Royal Glynneath Golf Club, playing off a handicap of 16.5, Mr Max Boyce!'

There was genuine applause and some cheering when I stepped onto the first tee. To all intents and purposes I looked like a proficient golfer. I had a bag with my name on it, FootJoy shoes, a Pringle cashmere sweater, a Big Bertha driver and a special 60° pitching wedge given to me as a gift from Slazenger for speaking at their company golf day dinner.

Now Seve at this time was endorsing all Slazenger products and his lovely flowing signature was engraved on the back of every Slazenger club.

The marketing manager of Slazenger explained to me how proud they were to have Seve endorsing their products and how he had filed his pitching wedge down to a razor's edge to cut through the turf on links courses.

So when I took my wedge out of my bag I was even more anxious to do well and impress the great man – a man I had watched win the Open at St Andrews and for whom I had unashamedly cried when he embraced the Claret Jug.

I pushed a tee peg into the firm ground and tried to place the ball . . . but my hands were shaking so much I couldn't get the ball to stay on the tee . . . and a WAG at the side of the tee cruelly shouted, 'Difficult course, isn't it, Max . . . !'

Finally I was able to address the ball . . . There were hundreds of people three deep peering over aluminium barricades waiting to take photographs at the top of my swing that Peter Alliss, that doyen of sports commentators, described as somewhat agricultural.

I was so nervous as I shouted to warn all the gallery, 'Watch yourselves, this could go anywhere.'

No one listened, some even laughed . . . but not for long . . .

When I finally swung the club, my Big Bertha driver . . . there were shouts of 'FORE!!' and . . . Jesus Christ . . . People began scattering everywhere.

An Epson steward in a high vis vest took to a megaphone and started shouting instructions. 'Don't panic . . . Please don't panic. Attention please . . . Please don't panic. Make your way to the fairways . . . You'll be safe there!' Grown men were trampling over women and children to get to the marker post . . .

Seve just shrugged his shoulders and said, 'Hit another one . . . It'll take a badger to find that . . . !'

While everyone was looking for my ball in the car park, I hit a little five wood down the long par five . . . and I was on my way.

On the seventh hole, a BBC cameraman who'd watched me have a little altercation with some ancient chestnut trees that line the fairways at St Pierre asked Seve, 'How's Max playing?'

Seve replied . . .

'Mac . . . he no play very well . . . He hit more conkers than fairways!'

Things went from bad to worse and I never wanted to play in a pro/am ever again.

As we walked off the eighteenth green, Seve said to me, 'Mac . . . give me your wedge . . . We go to the pro shop and maybe borrow a file.'

I thought, 'Oh, my God, he's going to file my wedge down to a razor's edge . . . like his . . . Oh, my God. We'll put it in a glass case in Glynneath Golf Club and have a competition called Seve's Wedge, and golfers will play annually for this unique trophy for as long as golf is played in the village.' My eyes were filled with tears.

Seve borrowed a file in the pro-shop, tightened my wedge in a vice . . . *and filed his name off my club*.

THE MAX BOYCE CLASSIC

In 1985, I helped organise a celebrity golf tournament at Glynneath Golf Club and called it 'The Max Boyce Classic'.

I was so thrilled to see so many greats from the world of show business and sport accept my invitation, which read,

You may have played St Mellion's, the course that 'Jack' built.
But have you played 'Royal' Glynneath, the course that 'God' built?

We had an incredible list of celebrities who agreed to play: Ian Woosnam, Ian Botham, Brian Huggett, 'Lynn the Leap', Gareth Edwards, Barry John, Mike England, Emlyn Hughes, David Gower, Hale and Pace, Jasper Carrott and a host of other A-list celebrities too numerous to mention.

The day dawned with lashing rain driving up the Neath Valley. The A465 was closed and there was widespread flooding. The greens that had been so lovingly and meticulously prepared over so many weeks were completely underwater and unplayable.

Sir Ian Botham played three holes in his underpants much to the delight and shame of the Ladies Committee and Captain.

After twelve holes of impossible playing conditions we were forced to abandon the event . . . I was heartbroken.

Now, Glynneath Golf Club at the time was not blessed with the greatest of facilities, and we only had three showers that were working properly.

This caused a huge problem with 150 golfers leaving the course at the same time all soaked to the skin carrying broken spindly umbrellas and sodden wet suits.

An old family friend, David 'Dai' Knoyle, who was caddying for Barry John, suggested to Barry, 'Come and have a bath and a shower at my house, Barry. I only live at the bottom of the hill.'

Barry John was very grateful and followed Dai to his house.

Dai ran a bath for Barry and gave him some dry towels. He then went on the phone to his father, George.

'George . . . Dad . . . Give a guess who I've got in the bath . . . *Barry John*.'

'Oh! Good God,' said George. 'Don't let the water out . . . We'll bottle it . . .!'

No one that played or was there on that day will ever forget the heady atmosphere that was created in the clubhouse afterwards, with Kenny Lynch singing 'Raindrops Keep Falling On My Head' . . .

They all felt so sorry for me that they all swore they'd return next year and do it all again.

Everyone kept their promise and got to finally play 'The Royal' . . . the course that God built.

It was simply an unforgettable day. Tony Lewis, the ex-England cricket captain, wrote a lovely piece in the *Independent* called 'Underwater Golf' and pointed out that only Jacques Cousteau had refused to play that day . . . claiming it was *too* wet . . .

BECKY

One of the most enjoyable weeks I have ever spent was in Augusta in Georgia at the Masters golf tournament.

Ian Woosnam, a past winner in 1991, invited myself, Sir Stanley Thomas (Stan the Pies) and Ian Botham to watch the greatest golfers in the world compete for the coveted green jacket.

Tickets for any one of the majors are incredibly difficult to obtain and are handed down from generation to generation. Die-hard golf fans on the last day of the tournament were paying $100 for 'spent' tickets to wear in their golf hats as status symbols.

We were all very excited at the thought of going to the Masters, albeit 'outside the ropes', when Ian Woosnam informed us that his wife, Glendryth, had unfortunately suffered a family bereavement and she and their children, Amy and Rebecca, would now not be able to travel.

Ian Woosnam then offered us the 'family' tickets, which allowed us access to the clubhouse and to '*All Areas*'.

Wearing our coveted and precious 'accreditation' plastic badge we walked down the famous Magnolia Lane to an entrance that said,

Players and Accreditation Holders Only

We approached the security guard, who was sat in a wooden hut unsmiling behind a steel iron-grilled window. He was an enormous man with a sheriff's hat and badge and a . . . gun.

'Hi there, you guys. How you all doin'? You got your badges?'

'Yes!' I said and showed him my accreditation.

'Glendryth Woosnam. That's a strange name. Never heard of that before . . .'

'It's Celtic . . .' I said.

'Okay, let's see if you're on my manifest. Glendryth Woosnam, number 135. That checks out. Have a nice day.'

Stan was up before him next.

'Name, sir?'

'Amy,' said Stan rather sheepishly.

'Amy! . . . That's a strange name for a guy . . .'

'Yes,' said Stan. 'My mother was expecting a girl.'

'Let's have a look . . . Yes, there you are. Amy Woosnam, number 136. You have a nice day, Amy.'

Then Ian Botham stood in front of the sheriff . . . I had to look away.

'Name, sir!'

'Rebecca . . . !'

'Rebecca . . . Where do you get that name from?'

Well, by now we were safely behind the other side of security and we shouted at Ian (Becky) Botham.

'Becky! Becky . . . Do hurry. We've bought you a tutti frutti.'

Ian was steaming by now and shouted back at me, 'You wait till I get over there, I'll stuff that tutti frutti right up your ——.'

'Now, Becky,' said the sheriff. 'That's no way for a lady to speak, cussin' and all that.'

'And you can —— up as well,' said Becky . . .

'Run, Stan!' I said. 'Run . . .'

GOG AIR

For many years, people have been complaining about the road links between south and north Wales.

So regular commuters were thrilled to hear of a new airline, 'Gogledd Air', flying directly twice a day from Cardiff International Airport (CWL) to Anglesey (VLY).

Boing boing. 'Ladies and gentlemen, my name is Idris Hughes and may I, on behalf of the captain and crew, welcome you all on board this Boeing 747 "Gog Air" flight to Cardiff International Airport.

'Our flight time today will be one hour and we will be flying at an altitude of 35,000 feet.

'So in the interest of safety, please ensure your hand luggage is safely stored away, your seats are in the upright position and your seatbelts are securely fastened.

'So sit back and enjoy the flight, and thank you for flying with Gogledd Air (Gog Air).

'Cabin crew, doors to manual and prepare for take-off.'

We'd been flying for about twenty minutes when *boing boing* the intercom crackled into life.

'Hello, this is your captain speaking. I regret to inform you . . . One of our engines has gone down but there's no need to worry . . . We've still got three more . . . and they are very good engines.'

Ten minutes later. *Boing boing.* 'Hello, this is your captain speaking. I'm sorry to have to tell you that another one of our engines has gone down, but we are still making great time.'

Five minutes later. *Boing boing.* 'This is your captain speaking, and I'm sorry to interrupt your in-house entertainment . . . but another one of our engines has gone down . . . but we've still got one good engine and it's running well.'

A few minutes later. *Boing boing.* 'Can I have your attention, please. This is Idris Hughes, your flight attendant, speaking. I very much regret to have to inform you that our *last* engine has gone down . . . and . . . this is a recorded message.

'Will all South Walians who can speak Welsh and can swim . . . *ewch i llaw dde yr awyren* (go to the right-hand side of the aircraft), and will all South Walians who can't speak Welsh and can't swim . . . Thank you for flying Gog Air . . .'

THE ORIGINS OF KEEPING UP WITH THE JONESES

There were two families living in Pembrokeshire, both fiercely proud of their genealogy, who were constantly arguing and claiming that their respective families were the oldest and the most respected and admired in that lovely part of west Wales.

One was Huw Williams, who was something of an eccentric aristocratic gentleman farmer who had moved back to Wales from Kent and was fiercely proud of his Welsh heritage.

The other was Hywel Jones, a 'red-faced man from the steep green farms' whose family had farmed the hills for as long as he could remember.

As it turned out, Hywel's oldest son, Gareth, fell in love with Cerys, Mr Williams's youngest daughter, and they were to be married.

You can imagine the speeches at the wedding reception.

Mr Williams spoke first. Emboldened with wine, he welcomed Gareth into the family and went on to make extraordinary claims about his family's genealogy and their accrued wealth.

'You see, ladies and gentlemen, the Williamses are the oldest in Pembrokeshire . . . and one of the wealthiest.

'It is claimed that we arrived on these shores before the Norman Conquest and before the Vikings built their stone settlements with Preseli Stone as recorded in the Welsh chronicles *Annales Cambriae*.

'It is said that the Williams family were farming these fields before Julius Caesar arrived on these shores in 55 BC.

'It is even rumoured, and my family believe it to be true, that the Williams family arrived here on . . . *Noah's Ark*.'

All the guests gasped at these extraordinary claims, and clearly embarrassed young Cerys.

Then Hywel got slowly to his feet and spoke in his warm Welsh accent . . .

'*Annwyl gyfeillio*, dear friends, can I just say how much I enjoyed Mr Williams's speech and how I was taken somewhat aback by his revelations of how old his family is and that *they* had owned most of Pembrokeshire from the sea to the sky.

'We, the Jones family, can't lay claim to have settled here before the Norman Conquest, and we certainly can't argue to have been farming the land before Julius Caesar landed on these shores . . . and we certainly didn't arrive here on *Noah's Ark* . . . You see, Mr Williams, the Jones family always had a boat of their own . . . !!'

TO GOD

One day, in the post office in Glynneath just before Christmas, a letter arrived in the post box and on the envelope it just said,

To God

The postmistress, a small, kindly woman who always had a smile on her face, saw that the writing was of an elderly person so she opened the letter . . . It read,

Dear God,
My name is Elsie Davies. I'm 93 years old, I've got arthritis, I'm partially sighted and I'm waiting for a new hip.
Can you spare me 100 pounds *to see me through Christmas. I want to buy a little chicken, a bag of coal and some presents for my grandchildren and my pension is not due till after the holidays.*

The postmistress, who was a salt-of-the-earth type of person, felt sorry for Elsie and she started a collection.
Well, they collected £95 and sent it to Elsie at the address on the letter.
Two weeks later they had another letter delivered to the post office.

To God

The postmistress opened it, recognising the writing, and it said,

Dear God,
Thank you so much for the money but I think you ought to know . . . it was £5 short. I think it was that woman in the post office . . .

A TRAVESTY OF JUSTICE

In the colliery in my village every section of the workforce was represented by a 'committee man' who served as their spokesman in industrial disputes.

One day the colliers' committee man, Ben Thomas, went to see the manager, Mr Pocock with a 'case'.

'It's about one of the colliers,' Ben said. 'Mr Harries, the under manager, caught him sitting down in the roadway last Thursday having a drink of water and cropped him half a shift's wages. Now this particular man is the hardest working, most conscientious collier in the whole pit. He's first in the face in the morning, clears his own coal, then helps the older men in the gate end to clear theirs, then back with the timber boys to help with the supplies.

'The man never never stops, and last week Mr Harries caught him having two minutes' rest and cropped him half a shift's wages. I think it's a travesty of justice, Mr Pocock.'

Mr Pocock rose slowly to his feet and said, 'I agree, Ben – I'm so glad you've brought this case to me attention, but don't worry, I'll see this man right, tell him to come and see me.'

And Ben said, 'Here I am, Mr Pocock.'

FROM *IN THE MAD PURSUIT* *OF APPLAUSE*

Little did I know what I was letting myself in for when I agreed to take part in a film about 'gridiron' football in America.

It followed Jasper Carrott's hilarious film by the same company, Opix Films, about his experience with an American soccer team called the Tampa Bay Rowdies.

The team we were to involve ourselves with was the Dallas Cowboys.

This was a few years before the sport had gained popularity in Great Britain, and the film was designed to explain, inform and generally whet the appetite of the new Channel 4 public.

I freely admit that at the time the Dallas Cowboys meant little to me, but the prospect of studying and getting to know the game in America intrigued me.

Such is the thoroughness of the Cowboys' system that before they agreed to the making of the film they wanted to establish my suitability. The Vice Chairman of the Dallas Cowboys, a Mr Joe Bailey, came to London and a lunch meeting was arranged. We talked and, loosened up by a few beers, shared a few stories.

I ended up much later learning a gridiron move or 'play' called *Blue Toss 39 Right on Two* which resulted in me 'rushing' eighty-five yards (after an interception outside Fenwicks) for a touch-down at the junction of Carlisle Street and Dean Street. Joe kicked the extra point.

Suitably impressed by my balanced running *and* my knowledge of real ale, he declared me suitable.

Later that week I met Gareth Edwards following the England–Wales rugby international at Twickenham. I mentioned that I was going to Dallas to have a look at American football and that I was desperately keen.

'Well, whatever you do, Max,' Gareth insisted, 'don't get involved.'

'But what if I train hard and lose weight?' I argued.

'You'll get killed.'

'But what if I take steroids?'

'They'll walk all over you.'

'But what if I paint a dragon on my helmet?'

'Ah!' said Gareth, weighing it up. 'That's different.'

I laughed and he wished me well.

Thus forewarned, the next week we flew into Dallas. I was interviewed on arrival by a local film crew, and in my eagerness to please, sang them a little ditty with a suitable Southern drawl.

> We flew into Dallas and I tell you all so far
> I ain't seen Miss Ellie yet and I sure ain't seen J.R.
> And I ain't been to Southfork, the ranch that's on TV,
> But I'm with the Dallas Cowboys and that's good enough for me.

They said I was 'kinda cute' and then enquired what position I was going to play.

I hadn't appreciated that the producer – because of his enthusiasm for the project – had omitted to tell them I had never seen, let alone played, American football. I wondered why many of them stared at me and slowly shook their heads.

They had understood that I was a well-known name in British rugby, but no one had told them in what capacity.

I kept hearing whispered conversations, and comments like 'He's kinda small, ain't he?'

After a few days' acclimatisation in Dallas I was asked to undertake a searching medical examination, including the delicate question of possible impotency. Apparently, this was not uncommon amongst gridiron players following long and rigorous weight training schedules.

After the medical, I was asked to go on a fifteen-mile run so that doctors could ascertain my physical condition on return.

When I did *eventually* return, my face like a red pepper, everyone had left the building, the place was in darkness and I was presumed lost . . .

The next day I was introduced to one of the coaches and given my play-book, the 'bible' of the gridiron player, where every set move or 'play' of the side was listed and diagramatically drawn. There were over 250 of these so-called 'plays', each of which had to be memorised perfectly.

Some of them were fairly straightforward, but others were incredibly complex and resembled a knitting pattern. I shuddered at the thought of playing a vitally important match, a 'play' being called by the quarter-back, and finding myself having to ask which one it was. I resolved I would learn as many as I could, and that night I went to sleep with the 'bible' by my bed.

After a few days in Dallas, which I found to be one of the friendliest places I have ever been and totally unlike its television image, we flew to the Dallas Cowboys' training camp in California.

The reason the training camp was in California, some thousand miles away, was because the intense heat in Texas at that time of the year made it quite unbearable.

The training camp used by the Cowboys was a college campus in the foothills of the mountains at a place called Thousand Oaks, some thirty miles north of Los Angeles.

I shall never forget that first morning being introduced as an *athlete*-cum-entertainer from *England* who was going to try out for the Cowboys.

I looked around at these huge men with some apprehension and wondered, 'What am I doing here?'

One of them approached me and said, 'You're kinda small to be in the trenches, ain't ya?'

I said, 'I haven't been very well . . . !'

He just smiled and said, 'You're gonna get worse . . .'

I was then taken to the kit room by a friendly Texan known as 'Cotton' because of his straw-coloured hair.

Unlike in most games, each player is allocated a number, and mine was to be ten, which I was thrilled about. I explained with boyish exuberance that this number had a special significance in

Wales, being the number worn by the outside-half in rugby, and that we had a great tradition of them with players like Cliff Morgan, Phil Bennett, Barry John, etc.

They looked blankly at me and obviously hadn't heard of any of the people I had mentioned – in fact knew virtually nothing about rugby football.

'Tell me, Max,' one asked. 'Why is it that people who play rugby haven't got any teeth?'

I answered, 'It's to stop them biting each other.'

He looked at me astonished. 'You don't say.'

They were without exception in total awe of rugby football, and kept saying they wouldn't dream of playing it.

'Those guys don't wear any pads.'

I was then given all the necessary protection, the huge shoulder pads, forearm pads, thigh pads, knee guards and my helmet. It had three or four steel bars forming a grille across the front, which I thought would have made it impossible to catch the ball or even to see it properly.

They explained it was a 'linebacker's' helmet (gridiron's equivalent of a front-row forward in rugby) and in that position the ball was purely incidental. I found it quite astonishing to be told that linebackers could go several seasons without handling the ball at all.

For my first few days I was to be part of the defensive line-up and to find out what it was like to be 'in the trenches'.

The first thing I was shown was a helmet slap, which in effect was a legal short-arm tackle delivered with the extended forearm to the side of the head.

I foolishly asked this huge player, a man of Irish extraction called 'Fitzy', to illustrate this. I was keen to know what degree of protection the helmet afforded. He chuckled, shrugged his shoulders and hit me clean over a bench into one of the changing lockers.

The film director shouted excitedly, 'Great! Great! Can we do that again on a wide angle . . . ?!!!'

Fitzy helped me out of the locker and enquired, 'You OK?'

He appeared slightly out of focus, but naturally I insisted that it hadn't hurt at all and that I was looking forward to playing 'in the trenches'!

Before each training session every player was taken to be weighed and strapped up. Every joint was strapped with tape to minimise the chance of injury. After my experience in the dressing-room, I was quite relieved to hear this and ended up some twenty minutes later resembling something from an Egyptian tomb. This, coupled with all the protective gear, made movement very restricted but after my flirtation with the locker I was quite prepared to put up with any discomfort.

This was the first time I had seen the rest of the 'rookies' – the other new players who were at the training camp hoping to become 'Dallas Cowboys'. There were some forty to fifty of these rookies, who had been 'drafted' from colleges all over America after being watched in college games by the network of Cowboy scouts that covered the whole country.

I found the method of drafting players fascinating. Apparently the side that finishes in bottom position in the league is given the first choice of new college players in the following season. The team finishing in first position in, say, a league of ten would be given the tenth choice, and then it's the turn of the side finishing last to choose their second player, and so on. This process is repeated until forty or so college players have been selected by each professional side.

This seemed a very democratic system and was similar to the way we chose teams as youngsters in the park or the school yard. There two captains were picked, a coin was tossed and whoever won had the choice of the best player.

Despite the undoubted fairness of this method of selection, it seemed to me a little harsh on the individual player's freedom of choice. I was also astonished to discover that, out of the forty or so college players selected by the Dallas Cowboys, only three or four on average would be retained at the end of the six weeks at training camp. They would then go on to become professional footballers with the Dallas Cowboys.

This, for many of the rookies, was to be the most important few weeks of their lives. For the established players, or 'veterans' as they were known, these rookies represented a threat to their place in the team.

Each morning would start with breakfast around eight o'clock and then we would be weighed and strapped up. Any player sustaining an injury through not having been strapped would automatically be fined. The morning session lasted from nine until twelve, and after lunch, vitamin pills and salt tablets there was a further afternoon session from two until around five. This was followed by a sort of night school from seven until nine, involving talks and lectures.

There was very little, if any, of the beer drinking associated with rugby football, and in fact most players were glad to be in bed by ten o'clock. However, coaches were sent around our 'dormitories' at ten to check if indeed we were 'home'. Any 'vet' not answering his late night call would be fined. There were occasions when some of the vets (whose place in the team was assured) never came 'home' at all and during the evening class of the next day were fined very heavily and subsequently disciplined (much to the joy of the rest of the squad).

In these evening classes I found it almost impossible to stay awake, not because I wasn't interested; I was so desperately tired.

The training schedule was carried out six days a week and subsequently I found myself absolutely shattered attempting to keep up with the other rookies, who were so much younger, fitter and stronger. They, meanwhile, came to look on me as something of an oddity, especially as a linebacker.

After the first week they had me lined up in a confrontation with Ed 'Too Tall' Jones, the biggest man I had ever seen, standing some six foot ten and built like a brick 'public convenience'. He was a living legend in American football, and was part of the Dallas Cowboys' famed and much feared 'Doomsday Defence'.

The coach rubbed me down, and whispered the play call 'on two'. This enabled me beforehand to know when to move. He would call some play like 'Delta Green Shotgun 85, 25 – Hut! Hut!'

The second time he called 'Hut' would be the signal for me to strike (i.e. on two). This is done in a game in an attempt to lure the opposition offside.

The coach said to me, 'Number Ten, I want you to walk all over him, hit him in the numbers, chew him up and spit him out!'

We went down into what American footballers call a three-point stance, a crouched position with one finger of one hand touching the ground, ready to spring forward. We were barely a yard apart. The other rookies looked on, whooping in delight and shouting encouragement.

'Go get him, Max. Haul his ass!'

The coach whispered, 'OK Number Ten, you ready?'

'Yeah,' I snarled, trying to look mean.

'Delta Green Shotgun 85, 25 – Hut! Hut! . . .'

I leapt at 'Too Tall' screaming, totally committed and determined to knock him over. He stopped me with one piston-like hand, picked me up above his head like a child – and dropped me to the ground in a heap. I picked my crumpled body up with tears in my eyes. The coach could hardly stop himself from laughing.

'What happened, Number Ten?'

'I slipped,' I said.

'Number Ten,' he went on. 'You're the waste of a good helmet! You're too old, too slow and too small.'

'Don't mess about, coach,' I replied. 'Give it to me straight!'

'You just ain't gonna make it with us. You better try somewhere else.'

I slunk away, shouting back to him in a choked voice, 'You wait till I paint a dragon on my helmet . . . !'

I lay awake that night and wrote some words to a song:

> Now I know this game is hard and rough,
> And maybe I ain't big enough,
> And maybe my best days are gone,
> But I'm the kind of guy who ain't afraid to try,
> Even if I die – with my boots on . . . !

In those first couple of days a few other rookies were discarded, or 'cut', and this would be the pattern at the end of each week until the squad was whittled right down. Those who had not impressed or reached the necessary standard were informed, 'Mr Landry would like to see you, bring your play-book.'

Mr Landry was the head coach, and arguably the most famous in America. He was always dressed in a sombre suit and a trilby hat, and never smiled. These rookies were taken to see him and it was explained to them why they had been cut. They then just simply packed their things and returned home.

For those boys, who had set their hearts on becoming pro footballers with the Cowboys, this was a traumatic experience and reduced many of them to tears. Some were cut only days before the end of training camp. To these players who had so nearly made it, it was particularly distressing, and I felt desperately sorry for them.

What I found astonishing was the fact that those who had failed to make it just returned to normal occupations and never ever played football again. Gridiron football after college is a professional game, and there just aren't any amateur teams. If you make it you stand the chance of fame and fortune. If you don't, it's back to relative obscurity.

This threat hanging over the rookies destroyed some players while bringing out a steely strength in some other less gifted ones. It also created a bond between us, which invariably happens in shared adversity, and I was thrilled to hear the other rookies pick up a simple little song of resolve I had written. The chorus of which went:

> All the rookies sing this song,
> We're gonna sing it all night long.
> We don't wanna get Cut! Cut! Cut!,
> We just wanna go Hut! Hut! Hut!

After my ordeal in the trenches I was relieved to hear that the following week I was to try out in a position called 'punt receiver'. This specialised position required the ability to catch unerringly the high ball following a kick-off (and run until you're flattened . . .).

I was fairly optimistic I would be able to acquit myself reasonably in this position, as it required no great strength or size. I had never been a great rugby player, but I had always possessed a safe pair of hands, whether it was at full-back or patrolling the long-leg boundary in cricket. After my disastrous first few days I looked forward to this new challenge.

The second week of training camp saw the arrival of more of the established players, and the crowd watching the training sessions grew to well over a thousand.

I was introduced to the punt receiver coach (each position had its own coach) who was to gauge my potential. I was taken to an area near the crowd and showed this contraption, a machine which resembled a cannon and was used to simulate a high kick. The ball was thrust down the snout of the barrel of this cannon and fired towards the waiting catcher or punt receiver.

There were certain adjustments that could be made to the machine that altered the ball's flight, height and range, thus making it more or less difficult for the catcher.

I watched them operate this machine and marvelled as my fellow punt receivers caught everything the cannon fired at them, equipped as they were with the special open face or single grille helmet.

It then came to my turn . . .

Because it was being filmed, and because of the cannon operator's inane sense of humour, he adjusted the machine so that there was maximum height and velocity and also ensured that it would spin in flight.

I stood waiting nervously some forty yards away, squinting through the grille of my linebacker's helmet. I prepared myself mentally and loosened up with a few simple stretching exercises.

'Ready Number Ten, here it comes.'

Whoosh – the ball was released. I watched it climb to an enormous height in a great curving arc. l ran forward to take the catch, squinting at the sky, my eyes filling with tears from the blinding glare of the sun. What made it even more difficult was my linebacker's helmet, which was totally unsuitable, and I cursed the protective grille. Then the ball began its descent. I had lost sight of it completely by now and just prayed it would somehow land in my waiting arms.

It fell from the sky (so I'm told) like a stone and dropped directly on top of my helmet. I was knocked over, and the ball, so I'm reliably informed, bounced some forty yards into the arms of a spectator.

'Nice trick, Number Ten,' said one of the watching coaches.

'Good header, Max,' said our sound recordist.

Our film cameraman, a certain Gerry Hall, was helpless with laughter and collapsed to the ground. Mercifully for me, because of this, the film footage was never shown on television.

It was explained to me later that it was common practice to look away from the bright sun for *some* of the duration of the ball's flight, hazard a guess as to the ball's direction and then look up again to take the catch.

I attempted a further ten of these 'launches' and was successful with only two. When I finally caught one cleanly after several attempts the big watching crowd gave me a resounding cheer and I punched the air as if I'd sunk a forty-foot putt to win the British Open.

However, one dour, humourless spectator and obviously avid Cowboy fan walked over to me. He had no way of knowing who I was or what we were doing. He assumed quite naturally that I was a serious contender for the vacant Dallas Cowboys punt receiver position. He came up to me and said, 'You're shit man!!!'

I tried various other positions that week and fared a little better as a 'punter' and as a 'kicker'. I found the ball was a little smaller than a conventional rugby ball and much harder. It was therefore much more difficult to kick. However, I did manage to get a 'hang time' of 5.001 seconds (the length of time the ball was in the air). Anything less than five seconds for the other rookie kickers would result in them being sent home.

The Dallas Cowboys' kicker was Raphael Septien, and I very rarely saw him miss a kick, even in practice. It was he who introduced me to the 'time capsule', a long cylindrical container filled with a heavy saline solution. Players who had had insufficient rest or sleep would lie floating horizontally in the container. The container door would be closed and the player left in an inky blackness and complete and utter silence. (Apparently it was impossible to sink.) It was claimed that an hour of sleep in this revolutionary way was equal to eight or ten hours' normal sleep.

I hesitantly crawled in and lay there for what seemed hours but, perhaps because of a long-time fear of drowning, I emerged an hour later completely covered in white crystals and not having slept a wink.

By this time it had been explained to the producer of the film that it would not be possible for me to take any active part in any real game, practice or otherwise.

However one chance happening changed all that.

I had spent a bruising and frustrating morning with the linebackers, who were working out with the tackling bag. This was a great heavy bag (similar to the ones used by boxers) with which these huge men, many of them weighing over twenty stone, practised tackling. They would charge rhino-like at the bag, lower their shoulder and drive it back against a huge coiled spring until it locked on to a ratchet on the end of a long shaft.

Failing to drive the bag fully to the end of this very powerful spring resulted in the spring recoiling the player back.

Even for these big men it required a great deal of effort, but for me, weighing as I did then around one hundred and fifty pounds, it was almost impossible.

I watched them run at the bag from around five yards, drop their shoulders and drive it jolting back. To have any chance I had to run at it from a good twenty yards, gathering momentum like a runaway goods van before hurling myself at this bag, much to the delight of the rest of the squad.

I very nearly managed to power it back fully, but then found myself thrown back, and ridiculed by the other players and taunted with shouts of 'Go practise with a bean bag, Max!'

This of course was followed with howls of laughter.

Later that night I returned alone to the deserted training area, which was well away from the main campus where the other players were resting.

I practised hitting the bag back time and time again until I managed to drive it all the way back against the spring.

Coach Landry, who, unknown to me and just by chance, had been walking that way, heard the 'jolts' of the steel apparatus and came over to see me.

He looked at me and, with almost a trace of a smile, said, 'You watch you don't bust that bag, Number Ten.'

From that one chance moment, I had gained his respect and he allowed us every facility and help, even suggesting I might make it to the first pre-season friendly at Texas Stadium back in Dallas.

He suggested I should try out as a running back (which is the equivalent of a centre in rugby).

'All you gotta do is run hard, run low and watch out for the big guys.'

The running back coach taught me a few plays and eventually we settled on one, a simple play called 'Blue Toss 39 Right'.

This was my invitation into a proper game, albeit in training.

The centre would snap it back to the quarterback, who would throw a lateral pass to me, by which time a 'crack' should have appeared in the opposition's defence (created for me by the blockers). I was then to accelerate through for a possible touch-down . . . !!!

I asked the coach how much of a gap would there be and was told: 'All you need, Max, is *eight inches of daylight*.'

We took up our offensive line-up position, did the famous Dallas Cowboy Shuffle, and then the quarterback called the play Blue Toss 39 Right – Hut! Hut!

The ball was snapped back, the quarterback took it and threw a lovely spiralling pass to me. Mercifully I took it cleanly and ran to the right, looking for the promised 'crack' in the opposition's defence.

Admittedly I did see it, albeit briefly, and then it 'healed' up again.

I was now looking for any way through, and driven only by instinct. I sidestepped this twenty stone 'defensive end' who was bearing down on me and then sheer fright slanted me, Barry John style, past another, only to be flattened from behind.

I had gained *two whole yards* – and dislocated three fingers.

The coach called me over and said, 'Number Ten, what you did there, you can't teach. That ain't in any coaching manual. You cut back against the grain and caused a lot of people to miss. Do you know that?'

I knew he wasn't serious but I still felt elated, I had gained *two whole yards* and I showed off my dislocated fingers like a child with a cut knee. I didn't dare complain, however, for I had been told: 'You have to learn to play with pain.'

'What happened to the eight inches of daylight?' I asked.

'It was there, Number Ten – it was there! But they saw you's a coming, and switched it off.'

However, I had impressed enough for them to persevere with this new 'running back' (even if it was just for the sake of the film). I went to sleep that night with a deep feeling of satisfaction that they had at last found a place for me.

We were now in the last few days of training camp and the rookies had been reduced to about five (and me). Training became even harder and more involved, with each session being videoed to be re-run and analysed later that night. I particularly hated the ten gruelling hundred-yard sprints in full gear that ended each session. However, I had now lost a stone and a half and was considerably stronger and fitter.

At the end of the week I was sad to leave the campus where I had experienced so much over the weeks. We headed back to Dallas to prepare for the first pre-season game against the Green Bay Packers.

I was astounded to learn that all the tickets for this game and all the other Dallas Cowboy games for the rest of the season were already sold out. I began to feel very nervous at the thought of playing in front of 75,000 people (none of whom had ever heard of me . . . !).

The plan was that if the Cowboys were leading by a sufficient margin with minutes to go, I was to run the last few plays including the play I had made my own – 'Blue Toss 39 Right on Two'.

I hardly slept the night before the game, and when I did I dreamt only of making seventy-five-yard touch-downs. The morning came eventually. I couldn't wait to get to the ground.

I felt nervous as I changed into my uniform. I asked one of the linebackers to adjust the straps on my helmet, and he locked it on tightly. I thanked him and explained that it had never fitted properly and the last thing I wanted was to have my helmet moving about. Especially if I was hit hard about the head.

Before the game, coach Landry gave us a brief talk. No one moved, and no one said a word. He spoke quietly in a voice that penetrated everything and everybody.

'OK, we are all prepared, but before I send you out there, I'm going to give you all a minute with your maker . . .'

Every member of the team knelt.

Seeing all these big men with huge shoulder pads, kneeling quietly in prayer, touched me deeply and seemed somehow unreal. Then in all that stillness coach Landry spoke to me, his voice reverberating around the room.

'Number Ten, take your helmet off!'

I mumbled an apology and fumbled with the tightly drawn straps. I felt so embarrassed as the whole team, God, and coach Landry waited for me to remove my helmet.

We eventually took the field, each member of the 'offence' was introduced individually to the huge adoring popcorned crowd. The commentator's voice boomed out over the P.A. system.

'Wearing Number 86 from Michigan State – Butch Johnston.'

The crowd roared their approval, and the lines of cheerleaders high-kicked their appreciation, balloons burst and the band played.

'Wearing Number 33 – Tony Dorsett.'

The crowd erupted once more.

Then it came to my turn.

'Wearing Number Ten, from Trefforest School of Mines – Wales – Running Back – Max Boyce.'

I ran on, waving to the crowd, hoping I wouldn't trip over, in my unashamed excitement.

The crowd roared, and then turned to each other and asked, 'Who the f . . . . that?'

I was made very welcome by the rest of the 'offence' and did the customary 'high five' hand-slapping routine. I then retired to the bench on the sidelines and waited my call . . . and waited and waited.

I watched the twists and turns of the Cowboys' fortunes and saw them unaccountably fall behind in a game they had been expected to win easily. I sat there for over three hours, in a confused state of expectancy, nervous apprehension and hope, trying to appear unconcerned.

When the final whistle blew, the Cowboys having lost narrowly, I was totally exhausted, and bitterly disappointed. The crowd hadn't seen my 'Blue Toss 39'.

I subsequently wrote this song to accompany the sad ending to the film:

Hey! Mr Landry, I'm here, I'm Number Ten.
I'm just sitting waiting, you just tell me when,
I'll give them all a shock when they see me run amok.
There's a new kid on the block – Mr Landry.

Hey! Mr Landry, I'm still waiting for your call.
Can it be that you don't mean to use me after all?
It looks and seems to me, it's there for all to see,
You have no faith in me – Mr Landry.

Hey! Mr Landry, I'll be more than just dismayed.
What'll I tell my friends when they ask me how I played?
I'm not the best that's been, but I'm more than kinda keen,
I'm looking pretty mean – Mr Landry.

Hey! Mr Landry, I've been sitting here awhile.
I've been sitting hoping, trying hard to smile.
But you never gave me a chance,
Not so much as a second glance.
You never gave me a chance – Mr Landry.

Following the success of the American football film, Opix Films wanted to find another suitable adventure for me along the same lines. We had discussed various ideas and, while we were reliving the Dallas Cowboy experience one night, someone came up with 'rodeo'.

I laughed and explained at once I had always had a fear of horses ever since I went pony trekking down the Gower coast and flirted with a Ford Cortina on the B road to Oxwich. A friend of mine who was an accomplished horseman had persuaded me to come riding with him. He explained it was only a little more than pony trekking. He lent me all the correct clothing – jodhpurs, helmet, boots, etc. – and we arrived at this farm in the Gower near Swansea.

As the horses were being matched up to the prospective riders, my fears subsided. The horses were old and ponderous, with names like Daisy and Bluebell. I faked disappointment. Unfortunately the instructor registered this and said, 'It's all right, follow me.'

He took me to this corral where some other horses were kept. He had assumed, because of my attitude on seeing the older horses and my borrowed gear, that I too was an accomplished rider. He led this horse out and I feebly asked the instructor its name, expecting a Pip or another Bluebell.

'Geronimo,' he replied.

I shuddered.

'He can be a bit of a handful,' the instructor went on. 'Keep him on a tight rein.'

My friend helped me to mount up and adjusted the stirrups. I plodded off with the others down the path that led from the farm. It was all very pleasant and enjoyable until we came to where we had to cross the main road. All the other horses pulled up and began chewing and pulling at the long grass, respectful of the holiday traffic. Geronimo, however, went stubbornly on despite my frantic attempts to hold him back. His ears pricked up and we were away. I hung on grimly as we narrowly missed a car pulling a long caravan. The driver understandably shook his fist and frantically blew the car's horn, which only served to drive the horse even wilder. He galloped away down the steep woodland that led through the gorse and the bramble to Oxwich Bay, picking his way through a thicket of silver birch, seemingly bent on decapitating his rider on the branches of every low-hanging tree.

We arrived somehow at Oxwich Bay, where Geronimo thankfully slowed down and pulled up on the wet sand. I had been terrified, but somehow I had managed to stay on. The instructor arrived with the others some twenty minutes later, rode over to me and said, 'Take it easy on the way back – *some of these people haven't ridden before . . .*'

I swore there and then that I would never have anything to do with horses ever again.

The producer heard me out, but was not convinced. He continued to try to persuade me.

'It'll be the best thing you've ever tried,' he argued.

However, I still wasn't at all happy with the thought of riding wild horses, and asked for some time to think it over.

The very next morning the producer rang excitedly and said, 'We've managed to raise the money to film rodeo in Colorado, and the Professional Rodeo Cowboys' Association have agreed to take you on. We fly out a week tomorrow. It's to be a co-production with the BBC. What do you think?'

He admitted that a week was no time to prepare and that it was asking an awful lot. It could presumably also be very dangerous. Would I attempt it? Despite my genuine fears, I thrilled at the enormous challenge and agreed.

The BBC in Wales made immediate arrangements for me to have some lessons at a riding school near Caerphilly, a place called Graig Fawr Farm. The people that owned and ran the stables, a Mr and Mrs Dennis Jones and their sons, were warm, friendly people and tried to put me at ease. Mr Jones's son Andrew was to be my instructor. He stressed it normally took a year to learn to ride properly but he would do what he could in the few days that we had. He brought me a horse. I prayed it wouldn't be called Geronimo.

What followed proved to be one of the most embarrassing moments of my life. I had purposely worn jeans that day and found they were much too tight to enable me to mount the horse properly. Eventually we were forced to make use of a milk crate to enable me to mount my steed. As fate had it, some students from University College Cardiff were at the farm at the same time on a riding course. They recognised me 'astride my crate' and came over. They had been watching with great amusement as I tried to mount this great big horse, and asked what I was doing there. I filled with embarrassment as I stepped down from my crate and explained: '*I'm going to be a rodeo cowboy in Cheyenne.*'

A few looked at me disbelievingly, while others sniggered. One laughed and asked whether I was taking my crate as hand luggage.

Apart from that incident my first lesson was uneventful, and I agreed to return the next day and every day until I flew out to America. My instructor pushed me as hard as he could in the days that followed and, despite a few hard falls, I think he was pleased with my progress. I had now begun to enjoy riding and was secretly thrilled at the challenge. Deep down, however, there was a strange foreboding, for I knew in my heart that riding a 'coop' horse on a Caerphilly mountain was hardly preparation for Cheyenne.

My friends at the farm wished me well, and a week later I arrived in Colorado Springs together with the film crew. The next day we drove out to the ranch where I would be staying. It was owned by a Mr Harry Volt, one of the biggest stock contractors in America, who supplied bulls, horses and steers for all the big rodeos. He was a gruff but friendly man and instantly admonished me for my clothing, and particularly my 'fancy shoes'. Apparently the ranch, 'Rattlesnake Butte', was infested with rattlesnakes and cowboy boots were essential. I casually asked what would happen if you were bitten.

Harry Volt called out to the cowboys who worked for him to come over. They were called Mad Dog, Preacher Paul, Chuck and Brad.

'Boys, this is Max Boyce. He's a movie star from over there in England and he's gonna be making a movie here.'

I didn't dare correct him and felt so out of place in my Jaeger blazer and fawn trousers (which the director had insisted I should wear) and I knew how ridiculous I must have looked to these ranch hands.

'I want you boys to show him round and, Preacher Paul, get him some proper clothes. He looks like he's selling ice cream . . .'

Preacher Paul, a big, warm, friendly man who had been converted to Christianity during his time as a marine with the American navy in Vietnam, was to teach me to ride and help me live the life of a cowboy.

I explained that I had very little experience and, because of this, had been advised to wear ladies tights under my jeans to prevent my legs chafing on long rides.

He said, 'Tights? You mean pantyhose?'

'Yes,' I stammered. 'I think so.'

He thought for a while and then said, 'Yeah, we had a guy out here before from England who did that. We fed him with beans, he passed gas and blew his boots off . . . Besides, Max, I wouldn't like the other cowboys in the bunk-house to catch you wearing pantyhose. They're mean men. They ain't seen a woman in a long while, and what with your long eyelashes and them there pantyhose, I wouldn't like to be responsible.'

I laughed and warmed to the big man.

The other cowboys, especially Brad, were much quieter and hardly spoke at all. I, meanwhile, babbled away in my nervousness, anxious to make an impression, and made small talk which I invariably regretted the minute I'd started speaking. In my nervousness I tended to speak quickly and I doubted sometimes whether they could understand me.

One night, after listening to me a while, Mad Dog said, 'That sure is a strange accent, Max. You sound just like a Cherokee Indian.'

I soon found that riding Western style was completely different to riding in an English saddle, and therefore negated much of what I had learnt at Graig Fawr. I persevered, however, and soon was heading for my first round-up on a horse they'd given me called Smoke Signal.

I had expected everyone to be involved, but it was to be just Brad and myself. We started out at first light, to protect the horses from the heat of the day, and rode some thirty miles to a box canyon to gather a herd of wild horses and a few bulls and steers.

Brad positioned me at one end of the canyon and then drove the herd through. Unfortunately, some three or four bulls broke away from the main bunch and Brad rode after them, shouting to me to take the main herd back the way we had come. I continued to drive them slowly back along the dusty trail, terrified to alter my position relative to the herd for fear of losing control of them.

After about half a mile, I became less tense and started to relax, making suitable calls to the herd and slapping the side of my horse with my hat to drive a little calf along. I leant back in the saddle of my flea-bit grey, wishing those university students could see me now on my first 'gathering', driving a baying, bellowing herd of wild mustangs, steers and Brahma bulls down the dusty trail to Rattlesnake Butte. 'Clint Boyce, trail boss.'

Then Smoke Signal stepped in a prairie dog hole and stumbled, throwing me forward, clean over his head, and frightening the herd. They began to stampede and run in all directions, several wild-eyed horses hightailing it back the way we had just come. I was on the verge of panic, feeling both horrified and helpless, and it was several minutes before I remounted Smoke Signal. I attempted to get the herd back together, but it was hopeless. I succeeded with some, but the older, wilier animals had sensed my ineptitude and uncertainty and toyed with me like third-formers with a student teacher. A huge Brahma bull faced me defiantly, with one broken horn hanging uselessly by the side of his head. For one terrifying moment I was convinced he was going to charge, but then mercifully he turned and rejoined what was left of the herd.

I got back to the ranch eventually, soaked with perspiration and physically and mentally drained. I had lost five bulls, twenty-three horses and my hat. As I came back from the main corral I heard Brad returning. I rode over slowly and sheepishly explained what had happened. He looked at me for a long time and then said slowly:

'Max, there is one thing a cowboy should never lose and that's his hat. You see, Max, it keeps him from burning up, shields his eyes from the sun and holds water should he ever need it.'

I said, 'I'm sorry about the horses. I . . .'

He threw his head back and laughed. 'It's all right, boy, they're here.'

He had seen what had happened, ridden round in a circle and brought them all back, together with the strays he had rounded up.

As we rode back to the bunk-house, he tossed me my crumpled hat.

'Fancy a cold beer . . . ?'

Next morning the horses were branded and loaded into great wagons which would take them to the rodeo in Cheyenne.

> And I wondered next morning how wild horses feel
> To be hauled off to rodeos in cages of steel,
> Away from the mountains where once they ran free,
> For the sport and the pleasure of a cowboy like me.

My initiation into the competition side of rodeo began at the Professional Rodeo Cowboys' Association headquarters in Colorado Springs, where professional cowboys instructed me with the aid of a mechanical bull.

My first attempt to ride on this gyrating, jerking contraption nearly resulted in a dislocated neck and my right arm being ripped out of its socket.

The watching cowboys just laughed, shouting advice and slapping their sides.

'Keep your chin tucked in there, Max.'

'You got him Max, he's tiring . . .'

After several attempts I was convinced my right arm was several inches longer. (Would my suits ever fit me properly again?) However, I began to master the technique and wondered what resemblance it would have to a real bull.

Despite the fact that every bone in my body ached from my confrontation with the mechanical bull, I was to find that out the very next morning.

We were taken to a small ranch owned by a stock contractor called Swede. He was a kindly old man who had lived all his life with rodeo horses and bulls and supplied stock to the smaller rodeos. I liked him immediately. I sat enthralled as he told me hair-raising tales of the terrible injuries he had received. I was so taken with this utterly genuine old character that when he offered me some tobacco to chew I took some. I made the further mistake of saying (in foolish bravado), 'It's good . . .' and then swallowed some . . . I turned away as my eyes watered and was very nearly sick, but I wasn't going to show old Swede. He brought me some every day after that!

So You Want to Be a Bullrider

'So you want to be a bullrider,
You want to be one too.
Well, I'm the only one who can teach you, son,
And I'll show you what to do.

'You just fill your mouth with marbles,'
That's what the old man said,
'Some orange, purple, blue and green,
Some yellow, white and red.'

So I did just as he'd told me,
Just as the old man said,
And I filled my mouth with marbles,
Some yellow, white and red.

'Then we'll enter every rodeo –
There's plenty here about –
And every time you see me ride
You spit a marble out.'

So we entered every rodeo
In towns I'd never seen –
Burlington and Henderson,
Cheyenne and Evergreen.

And I did just as he'd told me,
I rolled them marbles round,
And every time he rode a bull
A marble hit the ground.

Then came the day I had none left,
And I went and told him so.
He said, 'I guess you're ready then –
For the Pikes Peak Rodeo.

'Yeah! I guess you're ready now,
And your rope I'll gladly pull,
But you had to lose your marbles
'Fore I let you ride a bull.'

My first bull ride was one of the most exhilarating experiences of my life, and I shall never forget it as long as I live. I was very apprehensive, as indeed were all the television crew. The cowboys sensed this and assured me everything would be fine.

'Just cowboy it up, Max. You got enough want-to to make it.'

The bull they had selected for me to ride was called Smoky Joe, and I shuddered as I watched the cowboys drive him into one of the bucking chutes, his horns banging into the chute's timbered sides. I realised that now there was no going back, and worst of all, that *this* bull could not be set to buck slowly or for that matter be switched off at the mains.

A slow motion camera was located to one side of the arena while a second camera followed my fortunes in the chute area. The cowboys fitted some spurs to my boots and strapped a thick leather glove to my right hand.

'Okay now, Max, rub this resin in your glove and pull hard on this rope.'

The resin, through the friction of pulling, became tacky. This was done to help me grip the rope they would strap around the bull and prevent my hand from slipping.

The bull was still confined by the chute as I lowered myself quietly and gently on to his back. It bore no resemblance at all to sitting on the mechanical bull. The rolls of thick warm skin on the bull's back moved beneath me all the time and I nearly fell off in the chute.

The cowboys spoke quietly and earnestly and pulled the bucking rope tightly around the animal's back, trapping the back of my hand on to the bull. The loose end of the rope was then brought round for me to hold. My hand felt so tightly locked on that I was immediately filled with another fear. Would my hand be ripped off when the bull threw me? I shuddered at the thought. The cowboys assured me that this 'rarely' happened.

'Rarely,' I repeated, half choking.

'Normally what happens, Max, is when a rider gets thrown the lead bell weights attached to the rope drag the rope clear and release your hand.'

'Normally . . . ?'

The cowboys were now talking me through the preliminaries.

'Scoot up on his back, Max – That's it – Now lean a little forward – Keep your chin tucked right in – Lock yourself in there – Good – You just nod when you're ready. Wait till his head is facing straight ahead or to the left before you nod, or he won't see the chute open.'

My free hand gripped the side of the gate as the bull moved impatiently around, pinning my left leg hard against the chute sides. I was aware of the sweat that was running down my back and that my breathing came in short stabs. I clenched my teeth and gripped the bull with all my strength.

'You ready, Max?'

I was about to nod when –

'Hold it! Hold it! It's no good, we'll have to stop.'

The sound recordist had picked up aircraft noise overhead.

'Hold it everybody,' said the producer. 'Cut.'

I dismounted and found my legs giving way. I cursed the fact that they had to stop filming. I had built myself up to a real 'high' of concentration, only to be told, 'Sorry, sweetie, we'll have to do it again . . .' It was cruel luck, and left me physically and mentally drained and in a terrible temper.

It was a while before I was ready to remount the bull and start the slow build-up all over again. I begged the producer, 'Don't stop me this time, whatever happens. I don't care if a hundred helicopters fly over. Keep filming.'

He agreed.

Smoky Joe had become rather agitated by now at being confined in the chute for so long, and I was not at all welcome when I remounted. He stuck one horn into the side of the gate, splintering the timber, and clearly was not at all happy.

'Woah boy, stand back – Easy now.'

I waited until his head was in the right position . . . and nodded . . .

The gate was hauled open and the bull hurtled out of the chute. Although it was all happening so fast, I was instantly and acutely aware of the surging power of the animal beneath me as it bucked and twisted in an attempt to free itself of this appendage on its back. His very first buck had thrown me off balance and I clung on for dear life, all I had been taught forgotten.

He turned back to the right and bucked again, throwing me mercifully clear of his flying hooves.

'Stay down, Max!' the cowboys screamed. 'Stay down.'

The bull kicked high in the air, trying to rid itself of the kicking strap, and then turned back towards me. The cowboys moved between me and the bull and drove him back, snorting and kicking, to the relative freedom of his pen.

I had ridden my first bull.

The cowboys ran towards me, whooping with delight and shaking me warmly by the hand. I felt a tremendous feeling of elation and sense of achievement. I had stayed on for 1.6 seconds.

However short it had been, the sense of flirting on the cutting edge of danger had left me incredibly exhilarated, and all I wanted at that moment was to ride again. Tommy laughed and understood the way I felt.

'I was kinda hoping you'd feel that way, Max . . . It gets you that way, don't it?'

I was more relaxed on my second ride and not nearly as nervous. I had experienced it once and some of my fears had subsided. I was still surprised myself, however, to find I was eager to ride wild bulls. Another bull was driven into the chute.

'When you're ready, Max.'

I nodded.

The gate was flung open a second time. This bull was skinnier and easier to ride, and I stayed on for 4.1 seconds.

In my foolishness, I forgot to 'stay down' after being thrown and the bull's rear legs clipped my forehead as I got up. I had in my mistaken bravado come very close to being seriously injured or possibly killed. I went cold at the thought and hoped it was a lesson learnt. I was also quietly pleased that I'd ridden two bulls, and now began to feel a deep sense of relief and also genuine closeness to the cowboys who had befriended and cared for me and talked me through my first bull rides.

'Fancy a cold beer?' asked Tommy.

We went to a place where they served 'Surf and Turf'. I was told to order a 'T' bone steak – to get my own back . . .

Hey bull, I know you don't know me
I'm just a boy amongst men
I know you don't know me
But if you don't throw me
I'll never eat sirloin again . . .

That night I rang some dear friends back home and told them I'd ridden seven bulls and one for over two minutes . . .

The next day I was to try steer wrestling. This involved riding after a steer which had been released from a chute, throwing yourself from the horse, and wrestling the steer to the ground.

Seriously, for some unknown reason this held no fear for me, despite the fact that the bull riders were very apprehensive about me trying it because of the very real dangers involved. I agreed to practise on a plastic steer's head mounted on a bale of hay until I felt confident. I quite happily rode up to the bale of hay, threw myself at it with reckless abandon, grabbed the head's plastic horns and wrestled the steer to the ground. This produced gales of laughter from the watching cowboys, especially when I very nearly impaled myself on the steel spike attached to the plastic head.

I then attempted to wrestle a real steer and throw him to the ground. This was not easy and I struggled in vain with this poor creature, hoping I wasn't hurting him. Then along came the real thing.

The steer was driven into a little chute and I backed my horse alongside. When I was ready and in position, the steer was released and he shot forward (aided by a six-volt prod in his rear end). My horse charged after him until we drew alongside and I was looking down at the steer. It suddenly seemed a long way down and those horns I was supposed to grab hold of were real.

'Now, Max!' shouted the shoot man. 'Now! Jump!'

I leant out of my saddle until I was over the steer's back and then leapt. I touched one horn, albeit briefly, and then the steer stepped nimbly out of the path of my despairing lunge and I landed with a great thud in a cloud of dust. I was momentarily winded and felt a stabbing pain in my backside. I had landed directly on the steel battery case of the radio mike transmitter which was in my back pocket. Even to this day, I have a bruise which reads 'British Patent Pending No 4516/1'.

I attempted to bring down this animal several times, sometimes over-running the steer and being trampled on and other times missing him altogether. I was, after an hour, very sore, badly bruised, and desperately disappointed that I hadn't been able to wrestle the steer to the ground. I felt a little better about it later, when it was explained to me that it took months to be able to wrestle steers. I'd honestly thought it could be done in a single afternoon.

In the evening, I was taken to a masseur who attempted to get me into some sort of physical condition for the bare-back bronco riding that was scheduled for the next day. For the first time since I had arrived in Colorado I began to get a little disillusioned about wanting to become a cowboy, and asked the question:

> When will I get to ride off in the sunset,
> And hang around in smoky saloon bars?
> When will I get to draw and to tangle with the law,
> And sleep upon my saddle 'neath the stars?

Despite the massage, the tablets and the hot baths, I found when I awoke the next morning that every muscle in my body ached. I doubted very much whether I would be able to dress myself, let alone ride.

After a long discussion, the producer came up with an inspired suggestion: 'See how you feel when you get to the ranch.' Grimly I agreed.

The cowboys laughed when they saw me drag my aching body in, and suggested I'd be better off 'husk gathering in Arkansas' – which I took to be an insult.

'You have to learn to ride with pain, Max . . . What's the matter with you? Cowboy it up.'

At 10.30 I found myself back in the bucking chute, this time on a wild bare-back stallion called Steel. The procedure was the same as with the bulls: I was to nod when I was ready.

Despite my stiffness, I felt more at home on the horse, and a feeling of quiet resolve began to flow through me.

'Ready, Max?'

I nodded. The gate was hauled open once more.

The horse turned wild-eyed out of the chute and headed for the side of the corral with its high 'Kit Carson Fort' fences. I thought for one terrifying moment he was going to try and leap over, but he turned at the very last second, almost throwing me, and I hung perilously over the sharp pointed wall of logs that made up the fence. He continued galloping down the side of the arena and it was only sheer terror that kept me from being thrown.

I could hear the cowboys shouting and hollering, 'Hang on in there, Max! Stay with him!' And then I heard the most welcome sound I have ever heard. The sound of the buzzer that said I had stayed on for the required time. The horse continued to kick wildly, and then finally, as he turned at the end of the arena, sent me crashing into the wooden fence. Apart from a few scratches, I was unhurt and felt absolutely thrilled that I'd managed finally to complete an eight-second ride (albeit a rather ungainly one).

The cowboys rushed over to see if I was all right and shook me by the hand.

'Good ride. Good ride. You hung on in there.'

The old man who owned the little ranch rode over to me and said mockingly, 'Thought you said you could ride, boy. Seems to me the only thing you've ever ridden is a bar stool! We could tell what you was a-feeling when you heard that old hooter go . . . Shame you couldn't bottle it . . .'

After my week of intensive training, into which we'd crowded so much, it was decided that it would be impossible for me to compete in every rodeo event as was first hoped. I was to concentrate on becoming a bull rider – the one event that still filled me with apprehension.

Before that, however, I was to visit the most famous rodeo in America, Cheyenne Frontier Days, where I was to be taught some of the skills of a rodeo clown.

The rodeo in the old frontier town of Cheyenne was held once a year and lasted for a week. It was here where the most famous cowboys in America pitted their wits, their skills and courage against the finest animals for the highest purses.

It was a week when the normally quiet suburban town relived memories of the wild frontier days of the old West. In the daytime, as well as the main rodeo events, there were 'wild horse' and 'chuck wagon' racing, while the nights that followed were full of 'a-hooting and a-hollering' and the bars were full of fiddlers and banjo pickers playing country music.

Everyone was expected to dress the part, and you were not even allowed to order a drink in any downtown bar without a hat on. (This even applied to the BBC Wales executive producer, who decided for the week in Cheyenne that she should be called Sue – Teleri hardly being a suitable name . . .)

However, despite the hard drinking, there was very little real trouble and folk were right neighbourly. One night, when I ordered a drink (Red Eye naturally), the barman asked where I was from. I told him. He asked me what I did. I squinted my eyes and said, Clint Eastwood fashion, 'I'm a bull rider.'

He looked at me and said slowly, 'Bullshit . . .'

My first day at the rodeo I was introduced to some of the clowns, including a 'barrel man' by the name of Quail Dobbs.

It was explained to me that a 'barrel man' was more of an entertainer than the bull-fighting clowns, and I was to be made up as one.

Quail replaced my laughter lines with 'crow's feet', and fitted me with baggy pants, braces and a floppy hat. The barrel man, Quail, explained he was usually a funny old man built like a fire hydrant who jumped in and out of a padded steel barrel to entertain the crowd, and then braced himself inside it, curled up against the sides, while the bull tilted at it.

After a few disastrous attempts at jumping into the barrel 'butt' first, I managed it and looked forward with some excitement to my first day in the arena.

The other clowns were bull-fighting clowns, whose function it was to keep the bull away from the fallen rider.

They were also there in case the barrel should be knocked over and the open end left exposed to the bull's flying hooves and horns. Apparently, there had been cases where bulls had struck their horns into open-ended barrels – seriously injuring the barrel men.

This had not occurred to me . . . I was suddenly glad my smile was freshly painted and I couldn't help thinking . . .

I shouldn't be here
In this dusty arena.
Folks, I ain't all what you see
'Cos inside I'm shaking
With this chance that I'm taking –
This smile is just painted on me.

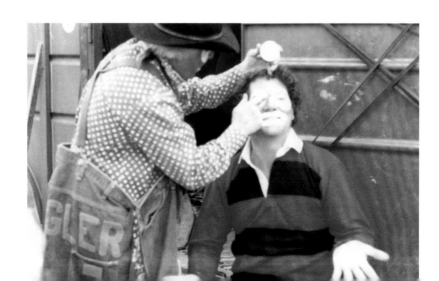

No, I shouldn't be here
In this dusty arena
With a smile from a tin on a shelf,
'Cos though fortune's beguiling
It's the paint that is smiling –
I'm none too happy myself . . .

The Bull-Fighting Rodeo Clown

CHORUS
The bull-fighting rodeo clown,
He travels to each Rodeo town
To be by your side when you're taking your ride,
The bull-fighting rodeo clown.

Now I've come to Wyoming to the town of Cheyenne,
Just another young cowboy to learn all I can,
To hear all the stories they tell in this town
Of the bull-fighter barrel man rodeo clown.

Now I watched a young cowboy 'fore he got on his ride
Tighten the rope on a Brahma bull's hide.
I watched him get thrown and his 'butt' hit the ground,
But the clown saved his life when he turned the bull round.

In their baggy old trousers, with their smiles and their
    jokes,
They greasepaint the day for the kids and their folks,
They brighten the dusty old frontier town,
The bull-fighting barrel man rodeo clowns.

Now a cowboy don't say much – it isn't his way –
Though the clown lays his life on the line every day
In every performance at each rodeo,
And he does it for cowboys he don't even know.

The bull-fighting rodeo clown,
He'll travel to reach rodeo town
To be by your side when there's nowhere to ride,
He's the bull-fighting rodeo clown.

My manager, Stuart Littlewood, who had just arrived from England that morning and had never seen a rodeo, was somewhat taken aback to see those great two-tonne Brahma bulls driven into the bucking chutes and his 'act' climbing into a barrel. He immediately left the arena and telephoned an insurance agent in Manchester (at three in the morning) to double my life insurance.

This in itself filled me with confidence, and I began to feel a little nervous about being in the confines of the barrel, especially as I'd heard the bull-fighters admit they wouldn't entertain it . . . 'If he sticks a horn in there . . .'

I was announced to the crowd over the tannoy and received a sympathetic round of applause. I jumped into the barrel and waited for the first bull to be released from the chutes. The tannoy crackled once more and echoed around the great arena:

'Wearing 151 . . . riding Moonstone – Brad Johnston.'

The barrel suddenly seemed much nearer the chutes and I hoped Stuart had managed to get through to England and to Manchester.

The bull turned out of Chute Three. He was a huge black Brahma with saliva streaming from his mouth and one broken horn hanging loosely at the side of his enormous head. The cowboy rode him well out of the chute but as the bull turned back to the left he kicked and twisted and bucked the young cowboy clear. The bull-fighting clowns moved in to protect the fallen rider, and he scrambled clear. I watched with horror as the bull then turned towards me. I shot down into the safety of the barrel and curled myself tightly against its sides bracing myself for the impact . . . There was none. The bull had run harmlessly past and was being herded in by the outriders back to the bull-pens.

'Okay, Max,' shouted the bull-fighting clowns. The tannoy crackled once more:

'Wearing number 253 . . . riding Lollipop – Randy Dwight.'

I began to relax and enjoy this 'close encounter', and was disappointed to be relieved by Quail after six bulls had been run and only one of them, disappointingly, had tilted at the barrel. For me it had been a bit of an anti-climax, but it had been a great opportunity to observe at close quarters the skills and courage of both rider and clown and the enormous, frightening power of these huge wild bulls.

Later that day I was discussing the day's filming with the director and the film crew outside the arena. I was still in my clown's clothes and said it was a pity, for the sake of the film, that I hadn't been hit harder when I was in the barrel.

As I was still speaking, people began screaming, clutching their children and running in all directions. 'Bull! Bull!' someone shouted hysterically. A huge Brahma had made an apparently impossible leap over the arena fence and was running amok outside the stadium.

People were falling over themselves in blind panic trying to get out of the path of the rampaging animal. I sought safety on top of a small caravan and watched three cowboys on horseback chasing the bull and attempting to lasso its back legs. They finally succeeded, and the terrified animal was led wild-eyed back to the pens.

The next thing I saw was one of our film crew waving frantically for help and shouting, 'Get an ambulance!'

Our production assistant, fifty-three-year-old Brenda Thomas, had been hit by the bull and was lying crumpled on the ground in an obvious state of shock. An ambulance arrived and Brenda was rushed to hospital, where they later informed us she had suspected broken ribs, heavy bruising, and had narrowly missed being killed.

The week following Cheyenne saw me teaming up with a bull rider by the name of Tommy Keith. I was to 'travel down the road' with him, gaining experience of the rodeo circuit before riding myself in my first big competition: the 'Pikes Peak or Bust' Rodeo in Colorado Springs.

In the run-up to my first appearance in rodeo competition it was decided for the purpose of the film to create a 'dream sequence'. I would be seen to be dreaming before my first competitive ride, and my fears and anxieties could manifest themselves in the dream.

I was to appear as an old bull rider turned mountain man who lived alone above the timber line in the Rocky Mountains above

Colorado. We hired bear skins, a racoon hat, moccasins and a bowie knife, and I lived the part for the days leading up to shooting the film. I used to check into hotels and the receptionist would say, 'Good evening and welcome to the Holiday Inn. Can I have your name, sir?'

I'd reply in a slow 'Jim Hardy' accent, 'I ain't got no name, but some folks call me Colorado . . .'

I had written a song called 'Colorado' to accompany the film, and one of the verses went:

> He was raised above the timber line, where nothing ever grows,
> But he was the only man alive who could ride old 'Crooked Nose'.
> He fished the mountain's clear streams . . .

The director decided he liked the song, and because of the storyline in the lyric he would film me fishing just below the timber line in the mountains above Colorado.

The only problem was that we had no tackle, and there could be no guarantee we would catch anything even if we had. It was therefore decided to buy some trout from a nearby restaurant and simulate the sequence of actually catching the fish.

We drove as far as we could along the twisting mountain road and then dragged all the heavy film equipment up the last few thousand feet to the lake of the summit. There was very little oxygen at this height, and we were all exhausted from the climb. We quickly set up for the sequence, with the director irritably hurrying us along because of the fading light.

'Max, go and unpack the trout and tie one on the end of this line . . . we're losing the light.'

I hurried to open the box and couldn't believe what I saw: the fish were *filleted*. We had no other option, however, but to carry on the best we could. We tried to keep the trout from 'opening out' by tying string around them, muddied so as not to show. We then filmed 'He fished the mountain's clear streams . . .'

We tried take after take of Colorado catching trout. It was absolutely hysterical as the first trout opened out on entry, the string snapped on the second one, and the third one broke in half and fell in.

The director, who was shouting at everybody by now and wringing his hands in despair, was finally happy with Take Twenty-Seven and I was covered in fish scales.

All this had been watched with growing interest by some other fishermen away on the other side of the lake, who were astounded at my good fortune and unconventional methods. They hadn't seen a fish rise all day, yet they had seen me land over twenty rainbow trout in as many minutes. Eventually curiosity got the better of them and they wandered over.

'Hi, there,' called this big Texan with all the gear imaginable strapped on him.

'Hey, I've been watching you – you're some fisherman. What's your name, son?'

I looked up and said, 'I ain't got no name but some folks call me Colorado.'

'Pleased to meet you, Colorado. Tell me what you are using for bait.'

I looked up, narrowed my eyes and said slowly, 'Just some old filleted rainbow . . .'

He blinked and said to his friend, 'Well, I'll be darned, I ain't heard o' that before.'

By now we'd lost the light and headed back down the mountain to drive to Colorado Springs, where I was to meet up again with the two bull riders, Tommy Keith and Brian.

While I had been away they had travelled thousands of miles, sometimes competing in rodeos as much as five hundred miles apart in the same day. I had experienced some of this lifestyle the week before, and tried to capture it in a song called 'This is the Life of a Rodeo Cowboy':

This Is the Life of a Rodeo Cowboy

Well, he'll wake up on some morning
In towns where he's a stranger,
In places where his stories and his songs don't seem to rhyme,
Where folk don't seem to miss him
And others just dismiss him
As just another cowboy, out of place and out of time.

But there's no burning daylight, it's time that he was leaving –
No time for hanging pictures, no time to loose the rein,
But he'll stop and ask a friend what he scored last night in Denver,
Grab a cup of coffee, then he's on the road again.

Sometimes he might win some, sometimes he'll get lucky,
Sometimes every cowboy has to learn to ride with pain,
But something deep inside him says 'Cowboy, you can ride him,'
And the hurt'll sit beside him when he's on the road again.

Sometimes he gets lonely and gets to thinking only
Of the ride he's got tomorrow – will he ever win again?
And his girl she thinks about him, in the time that she's without him,
And has she cause to doubt him when he's on the road again?

CHORUS
But his is the life of a rodeo cowboy,
This is the life, they say,
In a pair of faded jeans
And a rigging bag of dreams,
Travelling through the night to his eight-second day.

The next day, however, was to be my greatest test. The Pikes Peak or Bust Rodeo was the next biggest to the Cheyenne Frontier Days, and I began to get concerned about riding in actual competition, especially as Brian had told me that at least ten cowboys were killed riding bulls in competition the year before. He made me go cold all over when he described how two of his best friends had died and how he himself had got a bull's horn in his eye. One friend, he said, was stepped on and died instantly, and the other was run through by a long-horn. He described in detail how this young bull rider had then crawled back into the bucking chute to die, driven on by the adrenalin pumping in his already dead body.

I asked him why and how he could go on – after seeing his best friend die like that. 'At first I wanted to quit,' he said, 'and then it was as if Pete was telling me to carry on. He always used to wear a straw hat with a red bandanna and sometimes before I ride now I look up the stands and I swear I can see that 'straw'. I look again, and it's gone. I know he's up there some place and as to your question why I'm still riding, the answer is – *for the both of us, I guess.*'

We continued in silence after that. There was nothing more to say.

To Tommy rodeo was America's *truest* sport, partly because it had its origins way back in the pioneer days. It had been inherited from cowboys who had herded cattle on the great drives through the dusty frontier lands, and whose only break from tedium was

to pit their skill and craft against other outfits and other cowboys. Men like Tommy were part of a long tradition, and though sometimes they were 'out of place and out of time', they were proud to belong to a great heritage, and I was proud to have briefly touched it.

When we got to the rodeo the three of us sensed something was wrong. There was a silence and a lack of urgency about everything and everybody. Then we heard that in the opening event a seventeen-year-old girl had been thrown into a fence and killed.

Despite the terrible tragedy the organising committee decided the rodeo should carry on. In a rather subdued atmosphere at first, the steer wrestling, calf roping, bare-back and saddle-borne competitions took place. I watched without interest some of the rides and waited impatiently for the 'tour de force', the bull riding. This competition was always kept until last, to ensure that the crowd stayed on until the end of the rodeo day. The crowd buzzed with expectancy and I began to loosen up and do the stretching exercises I had been taught. I paid my entrance fee and shuddered when I heard the name of the bull I had drawn – he was called Bonecrusher. I swallowed hard and went to see him in the pens behind the chute. He was a lean, dark brown animal with long horns. I tried to look unconcerned, but my apprehension registered with Tommy, who took me to one side and said, 'It's OK, Max, I rode him once in Boulder. He ain't nothing special, he turns to the left and bucks a bit, that's all. You don't want any old corn husker from Arkansas your kids could ride. You won't win no silver buckles that way.'

We returned to the chute area and I began to get ready. I was the next but one to be announced, and I strove to prepare myself mentally for the ride. I was desperately anxious to do well and strode impatiently and nervously up and down the area behind the bucking chutes while Tommy prepared my rope. While I was going through these mental processes I heard a voice behind and someone tapping my shoulder. 'Hello, Max. I'm from Ammanford. How's it going?'

It was a man from south Wales who was on holiday in Colorado and had come to the rodeo for the day and read my story in the local paper. Normally I would have been glad to see him and made him feel welcome, but at that moment I needed to be alone with my thoughts – to concentrate on my ride. However, he went on: 'I think you know my Auntie Olwen . . . she used to work with you in the Metal Box . . . she was a checker on 'C' line . . . she says that . . .'

The tannoy crackled into life: 'Ladies and Gentlemen, the next rider out of Chute Number Four is Max Boyce. A month ago he hadn't ridden a horse, and now he's a bull rider. He's gonna be riding a mean son of a bitch by the name of Bonecrusher.'

I lowered myself down on to the bull, and Tommy adjusted my rope, offering advice at the same time. His voice was urgent now. 'Remember to keep your chin tucked in, Max. We won't let you go till you're good and ready.'

The announcer spoke again: 'Max has come all the way across the water from over there in England.'

'Wales!' yelled a voice from Ammanford. 'My Auntie Olwen . . .'

'It's his first ride in competition here in the Pikes Peak or Bust Rodeo – we wish him well. Let's hear it for Max Boyce.'

I waited nervously for the bull to be in the right position . . . and nodded.

The gate was hauled open and the bull turned quickly to the right, and once again I was instantly and acutely aware of the enormous surging power of these animals. I was terribly nervous, but coldly determined to hang on. I managed somehow to survive the first few crucial seconds without mishap, but then he bucked and turned hard back to his left, throwing me off balance.

The sudden weight transference caused the rope to slip, which left me hanging on perilously down one side, and with each twist and turn of the bull the rope slipped even further. I was now virtually upside down and becoming horribly aware of the bull's flying hooves. Only some basic primeval survival instinct kept me from being thrown.

I desperately tried to cling on but my weight became too much and I was forced to release the rope. As I fell from the side of the bull his hind legs caught me in the small of my back. A last contemptuous gesture.

The next thing I remember was the bull-fighting clowns sweeping the dust off me with a cane-brush and saying, 'Great ride, Max. You didn't tell us you was a trick-rider . . .'

I walked to the edge of the arena, my mind still racing, and tried to relive the ride. In all the noise and excitement I had not heard the buzzer and hadn't realised, until the other bull riders told me, that I had managed an eight-second ride.

I waited with the other bull riders for the marks to be read out.

'Before we have the wild horse race, here are the marks for the bull riding. Tommy Keith – 89 points.'

The crowd roared their approval.

'Clinton Husky – 75. Steve Whittle – 92. Local boy from here in Colorado Springs, Pete Brady – 95 points.'

The crowd erupted.

'And Max Boyce, who made us all laugh – 14 points.'

I knew my ride had been somewhat ungainly, but 14 . . . Apparently the judges marked for the style of the ride and not for the duration. I had come a creditable last. I was a little disappointed, but so thrilled I had managed to stay with Bonecrusher for eight whole precious seconds.

The cowboys were genuinely pleased for me and shook my hand warmly.

'Well done, Max, you had enough want-to to make it. You did all right.'

Then came another familiar voice: 'Hello, Max! Remember me – I'm from Ammanford. You used to work with my Auntie Olwen . . .'

I laughed and hugged him and told him his Auntie Olwen was the most wonderful woman in the whole world.

We left Colorado the next morning and said our fond farewells to the cowboys and clowns who had helped and cared for me. They were some of the most genuine people I have ever met. They were warm and friendly, honest and caring, and left a deep and lasting impression on me.

Following the success of the American football and rodeo series, Opix Films were always on the lookout for new adventures for me.

One day, they rang me up at home and asked whether I would be interested in playing polo on elephants. I laughed and didn't take them seriously as I had never even heard of such a game.

It transpired that they had been approached by Cartier, the jewellers, to film the 1985 World Elephant Polo Championship in Nepal and that if certain budgets and fees could be agreed they'd want me to be involved.

I was fascinated by the thought of going to Nepal and agreed on principle. I didn't really think it would ever happen and decided not to think any more of it.

A day before we were due to fly home from the Middle East I had a long phone call from the producer at Opix Films explaining that everything had been agreed and that I was to fly to Delhi and then on to Katmandu as soon as possible. The only problem, the producer explained, was the fact that I needed inoculation against the tropical diseases in the area.

The list was an alarmingly long one:

Yellow Fever

Malaria

Cholera

Typhoid

Tetanus

Luckily a friend of mine living in Dubai arranged for me to have all the necessary injections and I felt as if I was off to fight in Burma with the Chindits. The next morning both my arms were extremely sore and stiff and with a slight fever from the cholera injection nevertheless, I had to fly to Delhi to meet up with the film crew and the other members of the Cartier team,

who were Billy Connolly, Ringo Starr and his wife Barbara Bach.

Not even in my wildest dreams did I envisage that one day I would be flying to Delhi from the Middle East where I had been inoculated against cholera and yellow fever so that I could play polo on elephants with one of the Beatles.

Old Kathmandu was built for people not vehicles. Even cycle rickshaws, their rubber bulbed horns stridently tooting, were barely able to negotiate the throng of people crowding the narrow streets. Add to this the babble of tongues, the ringing of bells, the quarrelling of dogs, the chanting of prayers and the twittering of swallows and swifts. We watched them darting to nests beneath the eaves of the houses with intricately carved window frames splitting with age and decay.

It was an overwhelming experience. All one's senses and instincts were involved – including that of survival, since sacred cows and bulls roamed freely in the streets.

It seemed there were almost as many temples as houses, each temple complete with its wind bells, their chimes sounding man's devotion to his gods. We passed a fearsome black figure with six arms and a necklace of severed heads. It was the male consort of the god of destruction, whose wrath could only be placated with animal sacrifice.

A little further on we entered a small courtyard. The Kumari lived here, we were told. The Kumari is a young Newari girl selected to be the Virgin Goddess. The selection committee consists of priests and religious fathers. Likely candidates must first measure up to the thirty-two prescribed 'perfections', which include eyelashes like a cow's, stiff hair growing naturally to the right and a body shaped like a banyan tree. Young girls who possess these pre-requisites are then deliberately shut away in a dark room with recently severed heads from animal sacrifices and frightening noises which combine to shock and frighten the girls.

The new Kumari is easily singled out as the one who does not cry out or show signs of fear. Once discovered, the Virgin Goddess is taken to her residence where she remains until she sheds blood from a cut or from menstruation, thus showing herself to be only human.

I walked through the narrow crowded streets, rubbing shoulders with llamas and garlanded cows and inhaling smoke from incense sticks and butter lamps.

We were all enthralled and I longed to know more of their culture, traditions and history. The Nepalese people were gentle, smiling and friendly and had a wonderful religious tolerance towards each other. Buddhists worshipped freely at Hindu shrines. Then there were the children tugging shyly at our sleeves selling their little trinkets.

'Only one rupee . . . only one.'

I found it impossible to refuse them. The bangles and bracelets were hammered out of copper wire and brass. Our self-appointed guide, a young Nepalese boy, explained that I had bought enough bangles to ensure the telephone linesmen of Nepal would be working over the weekend. That evening, when I tried to ring home and repeatedly failed to get through, I realised why my only contact with the outside world was not working . . . I was wearing it.

We were sorry we had to leave this fascinating place, with its noise and bustle, its powder-sprinkled idols, where white was the colour of mourning, but we knew we could never see everything, no matter how long we stayed.

Leaving Kathmandu, we journeyed by Land Rover, through some of the wildest country I have ever seen, to the Tiger Tops jungle lodge, some fifty miles away in the Chitwan National Park. We followed the twisting mountain road through the terraced rice fields that were stepped into the hillside.

Set against the magnificent backdrop of the Himalayan Mountain Range, they reminded me of a great empty concert hall.

On the way we passed the simple peasant villages. They were undoubtedly the most primitive I have ever seen, but all the doorways were hung with offerings to the gods Vishnu and Shiva. However, the people and especially the children appeared so happy and ran out to us waving and smiling and calling, 'Bye Bye. Bye Bye', – apparently the only English word they know.

I watched them and marvelled at their inventiveness and the little games they played — one with berries and stones, and another where a piece of ripped tyre off a Land Rover became a ball, with cardboard as their bat.

I couldn't help but think, reflecting on their simple but seemingly so happy way of life, that *I was poorer by far*.

With a Round Stone and a Jar

On a mountain's empty concert hall,
I sat amongst the stalls
And wondered at this unspoilt land
Where the wild Trisuli sprawls,
And I watched the tin-sled buses
Winding through the afternoon
As the lines of silver paper
Sang an offering to the Moon.

And I heard the wind-bells' tinkling song
Played by the kindly breeze
And the prayer flags' gentle flutter
In a vain attempt to please,
And I longed to know these people's thoughts
As I watched them shyly stare
And wondered at this different faith
I found too late to share.

We rode on down that dusty road
Beneath the reddening skies,
And laughed as waving children
Turned hellos into goodbyes,
And I watched them play their simple games
With a round stone and a jar,
And I couldn't help but thinking
I was poorer by far.

And I wondered what they dreamt about
By their butter lamps at night
In their humble dwelling places
Where the wind blows out the light.
And did they dream of distant lands
Beyond the furthest star,
Where children play with berries,
A round stone and a jar?

After some four hours' driving we stopped to eat our packed lunch by the sprawling River Trisuli. We sat down on the banks of the river and watched some laughing children splashing and playing in the river. I went to take some photographs and to my horror found the naked body of a woman lying in the river. She had in her mouth a small piece of coal, which our guide explained was a symbolic act of cremation. Her family had cast her body traditionally to the river and because they were too poor to buy the necessary requirements for cremation they symbolised the act with the piece of coal. We were all deeply shocked, but our guide explained that it was not uncommon and to the people of this region death was no stranger.

We had no stomach for eating now, and we abandoned our lunch and drove on to the Chitwan National Park. We finally and thankfully arrived after the sixty-mile journey which had taken us over six hours, during which we were thrown about on the narrow twisting mountain roads with sheer drops on either side.

The jungle lodge was built on stilts and situated in the middle of dense jungle, which we were told was inhabited by several different forms of wildlife including tiger, rhino and crocodile. The lodge was very basic, with no electricity and no telephone.

The film crew were put up in tents near the lodge, and as darkness fell and the sounds of the jungle increased, no one slept easy. Every shadowy tree was a rhino, and every rustling sound a man-eating tiger.

Glenda, our production assistant, was not at all happy and was further distressed when she was shown a spider which measured some five inches across. Russ Walker, our cameraman, swore he saw one trying his trousers on . . . Glenda was not amused, and swore she'd never be able to close her eyes, let alone sleep.

The next morning we woke to find the lodge shrouded in mist and heard the laboured sound of the hand-driven pump as it clanked water to the few rooms of the jungle lodge.

I showered in freezing cold water, which was luxury compared with the film crew's bucket of water and a bar of green Lifebuoy soap left over from a Gurkha's First World War survival kit.

There were no toilet facilities other than the freedom of the Chitwan National Park. Despite the need for privacy the film crew never ventured far into the steamy jungle, preferring instead to answer the call of nature in a position of safety rather than decency.

We made our way by Land Rover and raft to the elephant polo ground. The raft was made from a hollowed-out tree, and its lowness in the water left us all a little concerned as we had been told the river was infested with crocodiles. Although we had also been told they were only fish eaters no one trailed their fingers in the water for fear the crocodiles might feel like a little change. (Any mishap would have resulted in the original fish finger . . .)

When we landed safely on the other side we had our first view of the elephants. They looked out of the mist like great grey ghosts slowly moving upstream to the polo field.

The mahoots were skilfully driving them, with their bare feet prodding and nudging behind the elephants' ears. The elephants were being taken to have patterns painted on them with coloured chalks, which gave them a startling new appearance.

I looked forward with boyish exuberance to our first game, which was to be against the Gurkhas. They were four commissioned senior officers who would not have looked out of place on the set of *The Jewel in the Crown*. They were friendly, but frightfully Army, and were obviously the last remnants of the Raj. They had of course played elephant polo before, spoke fluent Nepalese and had never lost a game.

We had been given a crash course on the rules of elephant polo, none of which made any sense to Billy, Ringo, Barbara or myself. We decided to play it cavalier fashion and throw caution to the winds. There was to be no game plan, and no elephant-to-elephant marking.

It soon became evident that the choice of polo sticks was of paramount importance. There were hundreds to choose from, all of different lengths and thicknesses. The slender ones were light but far too whippy, whilst the stiff-shafted ones proved impossible to swing. After much indecision we eventually chose the ones that fitted our elephants and felt most comfortable.

The mahoots instructed the elephants to sit, and we dragged ourselves on behind the mahoots by means of the ropes which served to keep us from falling off and as makeshift stirrups. We were effectively tied on to the elephants, which was just as well, for when they stood up the ground seemed a long way down.

After a few practice runs and tilts the referee, sitting astride a vast African elephant with huge tusks, blew the whistle to begin the first 'chukka'.

Barbara Bach drove her baby elephant forward and squealed her way to the first physical confrontation with the opposition – Brigadier Hunt-Davis of the 7th Gurkha Division. She reached the ball first, took an almighty swing and missed it by about two feet and nearly fell off. The Brigadier, urged on by his 'chaps', whacked it away from the centre spot and attacked down the left flank. He was doing rather well until his own personal stick was splintered out of his hand by a crushing Ian St Connolly tackle.

'I say, steady on old boy,' snorted the Brigadier.

Billy's answer was lost amongst the trumpeting of the elephants.

In his very first tackle of the World Polo Championships Billy had come close to being sent off and was fortunate to have escaped with only a caution.

The game was never going to be a classic and hardly pleased the connoisseur of elephant polo. Whatever the purist might say, however, there was a great deal of honest effort, much endeavour and intelligent running off the ball by Ringo Starr. Ringo undoubtedly was feeling the effects of an earlier tackle and would have been substituted had we had a substitute. He had what could only be described as an indifferent game and was guilty of a lot of loose play. He made no contact at all with the ball and was severely spoken to by the referee for accidentally whacking one of the opposition's elephants on the trunk. Something that had never been seen before at this level of polo.

Mercifully the whistle went for half-time and, such is the democratic and fair way the game is played, we swapped elephants. This proved our downfall, for elephants never forget, and the elephant Ringo had whacked was never quite the same again and certainly never at ease with Ringo astride him brandishing his stick like a shillelagh. Because of the elephant's understandable reluctance to 'get stuck in' we virtually played the second half with only three elephants.

Billy was magnificent at the heart of our defence and managed to terrify the Brigadier with his Hannibal-like charges, dislodging his stick and his pith helmet on frequent occasions. During a skirmish in front of goal my elephant actually stepped on the ball and buried it. Play was held up for several minutes while the ball was dug out and I was booked for time-wasting and ungentlemanly conduct. This break in play allowed the Gurkhas to regroup and to deploy some of their set-piece moves.

They were helped in no small measure by the fact that Ringo's elephant was fertilising a huge area outside the six-yard box and was unable to continue for several minutes. The Gurkhas inevitably scored and went on to win two-nil.

We returned to the Tiger Tops lodge, suitably chastened, in the late afternoon. We had just ordered some drinks when a bell rang out and the camp suddenly became a frantic hive of activity. The bell was a signal that a wild tiger had been lured to a part of the jungle where it could be seen and observed. It had been lured there by the staking out of live bait, which seemed cruel but apparently was essential. When the bell rang everyone ran in all directions in a frenzied dash so as not to miss the chance of seeing a tiger in its natural surroundings.

We clambered on to the Land Rovers, which drove part of the way into the jungle, and then we continued on foot. When we got nearer to where the tiger had taken the bait, we were asked in hushed whispers to remove our shoes and continue quietly in absolute and utter silence.

We all linked hands and were led in complete darkness through the dense jungle, not knowing where we were going or what was going to happen. I must admit at this stage I felt distinctly uneasy creeping through the jungle in bare feet, and had it not been for the silence imposed I would have casually said, 'I think I'll go back now – I'm not fussy if I see one or not.' (Later everybody else admitted to feeling the same.)

Suddenly we came into a clearing and were abruptly stopped, bumping into one another in the process amid stifled squeals and frightened giggles. Across the ravine we could see the tiger, lit by a small searchlight, tearing and gnawing at a young water buffalo it had just killed. The tiger was a fully grown male, and although it was a cruel and gruesome sight one couldn't help but marvel at this magnificent wild beast.

Meanwhile, back in the jungle lodge, an even more bizarre scene was being enacted. Steve Strange, the outrageous rock singer, had arrived from England to play in the polo and was sleeping off the effects of alcohol and the long flight, completely oblivious to the practice of baiting tigers and therefore totally unaware of why the bell was ringing. He lay in a deep sleep and wearing only his underpants. Then he was suddenly aware of someone banging on his door shouting excitedly 'Tiger! Tiger!' and people running in all directions.

He leapt to his feet wild-eyed and, naturally, terrified, expecting to see a maneater at the foot of the stairs.

'Tiger! Tiger!' shouted the young native boys. Steve began to run, not knowing from which direction the tiger was coming or where he was going.

'Tiger! Tiger! – quick sir,' pleaded one of the boys. Steve, mistaking the boy's genuine excitement for terror, grabbed hold of the bewildered youngster and fled with him to safety. The boy, not being able to speak English, was astonished to be carried off by this spiky-haired stranger in his underpants.

Steve, in all fairness, was intent on saving both their lives and, so the story goes, ended up on the roof of the jungle lodge with a terrified young Nepalese waiter.

'It's all right now, son,' said Steve, pacifying the boy. 'We'll be safe up here . . .'

AN AFTERTHOUGHT

This has been the anthology of some of my favourite poems, songs and stories.

They have taken me on a journey that I would never have envisaged or imagined. The way was not always easy and the climb was often steep but the view was ultimately worthwhile.

I realise some of my work has gathered dust on the shelves of time. They belong to an age that has passed, but I have included them for they are of a certain time and place that is worth remembering and precious to me.

I have placed them among more recent poems, songs and stories that were picked in the freshness of the morning, following the midnights of despair where I worried would I ever write anything of any significance again.

This then is the **Harvest of My Autumn** – one I have been privileged to share. It is late gathered but I hope all the richer for it.

M. B.
September 2021

ACKNOWLEDGEMENTS

My thanks to Stuart Littlewood for 'keeping on at me' to complete this book; to Carla, Jayne, Nicola and Siobhan for their research; to Michael McCarthy (Clonmel) for the Craic; to Phillip (5 to 12) Whitehead for The Road and the Miles; and to Paul Carman (P.C), my muse and confidant.

I also wish to express my gratitude to the illustrators Anne Cakebread, Fran Evans, Rhys Padarn Jones, Darryl Jones and my late friend Gren, for they have given my work another dimension.

And last but not least my thanks to all who inhabit this book, for you have been my inspiration.

Paul Carman (P.C),
my late long-term bass player

My long-serving band, L–R: Paul Smith, Peter King, Max Boyce, Jonathan Lewis, Dick Roberts